SCOTT M. FRALEY

AI for Beginners

A Practical Guide to Artificial Intelligence in Daily Life,
Real-World Applications, Ethics, and Future Trends

First edition

This book was professionally typeset on Reedsy.
Find out more at reedsy.com

Contents

Introduction

I magine waking up in a world seamlessly interwoven with technology that not only understands your needs but anticipates them. The day begins, and your smart device has already curated your morning playlist based on your mood from yesterday's digital interactions. As you sip your coffee, the newsfeed on your tablet summarises global updates tailored to your interests, highlighting essential developments in your field. This isn't a scene from a futuristic movie; it's a glimpse into our AI-driven reality—an era where artificial intelligence is at the helm of transforming how we live, work, and interact.

Artificial Intelligence, or AI, often mystified by its complex algorithms and tech jargon, is fundamentally reshaping countless aspects of our daily lives. From the autonomous vehicles navigating traffic with ease to virtual assistants simplifying tasks, AI's influence is undeniable. For a beginner stepping into this realm, the sheer scope of AI can seem overwhelming, yet its potential promises a frontier teeming with opportunities and innovations. Whether you're completely new to technology or a business professional eager to integrate AI into your work, understanding these principles equips you with a powerful toolset for the future.

This book aims to demystify AI, breaking down intricate concepts into relatable insights. It serves as your compass in unraveling the sophisticated tapestry of AI, guiding you from foundational knowledge to practical applications. By embarking on this journey, you'll discover not just what AI is, but how it poignantly intersects with both mundane routines and monumental career shifts. You'll learn to view AI not merely as a technical marvel but as an integral force capable of enriching every facet of human endeavor.

Why should anyone care about AI? The answer lies in its ubiquity and adaptability across various fields. Business sectors are harnessing AI to streamline operations, boost productivity, and spur innovation. As the market evolves, professionals equipped with AI literacy are better positioned to leverage these technologies for strategic outcomes. Entrepreneurs and freelancers find in AI a partner that can optimize workflows, offering competitive edges in a fast-paced digital marketplace. For students and tech enthusiasts, comprehending AI opens a gateway to dynamic career paths loaded with creativity and transformation.

Consider, for instance, the healthcare industry revolutionized by AI interventions. Algorithms predict patient diagnoses with stunning accuracy, augment clinical decisions, and personalize treatment plans. In finance, AI analyzes vast quantities of data to detect fraud, enhance decision-making, and forecast economic trends with incredible precision. Each chapter in this book unfolds new dimensions of AI's impact on such industries, drawing connections to its overarching relevance in enhancing societal progress.

Beyond industry-specific benefits, AI harbors the power to reshape our personal existence. It's not just about tech-savvy enterprises; it's about empowering individuals like you to embrace tools that render life more efficient and productive. From AI-powered learning platforms tailoring educational content to match individual learning speeds and styles to smart home devices conserving energy while optimizing comfort, the profound influence of AI is destined to touch every corner of daily living.

Another critical aspect explored involves understanding the ethical frameworks surrounding AI advancements. As these intelligent systems become more pervasive, the pertinent question arises: how do we manage this power responsibly? Ensuring fair, unbiased, and transparent AI practices becomes a core theme, urging readers to contemplate the ethical implications alongside the technological marvels. This book will navigate these waters, shedding light on balancing innovation with integrity.

As we delve further, each chapter will systematically uncover key themes and narratives shaping the AI landscape. You'll encounter user-friendly tools democratizing access to AI, catalyzing innovation for even those without technical expertise. We'll journey through startups harnessing AI to tackle pressing global issues, showcasing the humanitarian potential nested within these technologies. Furthermore, by assessing emerging trends, you will gain insight into how AI endeavors to evolve, shaping the next generation of technological milestones.

In preparing you for this voyage into the AI universe, this introduction aims not only to inform but also to inspire. It's an invitation to explore not just the practical mechanics of AI but to engage with its philosophical questions and transformative possibilities. With modern language and straightforward explanations tailored to your needs, consider this book your roadmap—a guide through the labyrinthine corridors of AI innovation and integration.

Ultimately, this endeavor seeks to illuminate a path wherein AI acts as an ally rather than an enigma, encouraging continuous learning and adaptation. Grasping these basics isn't just a step towards technical proficiency; it's embracing a mindset attuned to future growth and development. So whether you're driven by curiosity, professional ambition, or entrepreneurial zeal, this book is your launching pad into a world enriched by AI's promise and potential. Welcome to your first step into understanding AI's diverse and impactful cosmos, a journey designed to empower and elevate your skills and insights in the thriving digital age.

Chapter 1: Understanding AI: The Basics

U nderstanding AI is about grasping the basics of how machines simulate aspects of human intelligence. This fascinating area draws both tech enthusiasts and those new to the field, eager to explore how these digital systems mirror human problem-solving abilities. Whether it's a smartphone predicting your next text word or a virtual assistant providing directions, examples of AI emulating human cognition are growing increasingly common in our daily lives. These applications underscore a crucial point: AI does more than mimic human actions; it captures the essence of thought processes in a computational form. As we delve deeper into this topic, it becomes clear that the simulation of human intelligence extends beyond professional uses and is woven into personal technologies like smart home devices and voice recognition systems.

In this chapter, readers will journey through the foundational concepts of AI, a field that continues to redefine technological boundaries. We'll explore how AI integrates with everyday life through task automation, enhancing productivity by tackling mundane tasks previously handled by humans. You'll also discover the various types of AI, including Narrow AI which excels in specific tasks like image recognition, and General AI which aspires to think comprehensively like humans. By distinguishing between these types, we can understand current advancements and future potential impacts. Furthermore, we'll address widespread misconceptions that cloud public perception of AI, emphasizing the need for realistic expectations. Real-world examples will illustrate AI's role in revolutionizing industries and everyday routines, while discussions on ethical considerations will highlight the importance of responsible AI deployment. Through these topics, the chapter provides a comprehensive look at how AI is shaping technological innovation and societal change, making it an indispensable resource for beginners, business professionals, students, and entrepreneurs alike.

1.1 Defining Artificial Intelligence

Artificial intelligence (AI) is a fascinating field that captures the imagination of both tech enthusiasts and laypeople alike. To understand AI, one must first recognize its primary purpose: simulating human intelligence in machines to perform tasks usually requiring human intellect. This includes learning from experience, adapting to new inputs, and completing tasks typically associated with humans.

At its core, AI's goal is to build systems that mirror human problem-solving abilities. Imagine asking a virtual assistant like Siri for directions or having your smartphone predict the next word you're likely to type—these instances showcase how AI emulates aspects of human cognition. By doing so, AI aims to perform cognitive functions related to problem solving and decision making. This approach isn't just about mimicking human actions; it's about capturing the essence of human thought processes and applying them in a computational context. For instance, Deep Blue, the chess program created by IBM, demonstrated strategic thinking through AI when it defeated world champion Garry Kasparov in 1997, showcasing a machine's ability to tackle complex problems (Source 1).

Understanding AI also involves appreciating its integration into everyday life via task automation. Automation powered by AI impacts various mundane and repetitive activities, relieving humans from these tasks. Consider robotic process automation (RPA), which allows businesses to automate data entry tasks traditionally done by people. RPA's capabilities expand significantly when combined with AI, enabling it to handle more complex workflows and respond dynamically to changes. This seamless blend of AI in enhancing productivity showcases its profound implications on efficiency across industries.

Also crucial is recognizing AI's transformative impact on everyday interactions. Machine learning, a fundamental subset of AI, enables computers to learn from data, identify patterns, and make decisions with minimal human intervention. This is particularly evident in personalized recommendations you receive while shopping online or streaming content—AI algorithms analyze your behavior to suggest products or shows tailored to your preferences.

Generative AI takes this a step further by creating original content, including text, images, and music. For instance, platforms use deep learning approaches to generate realistic dialogues in chatbots, making conversations seem more human-like with each interaction. Such advancements highlight AI's role in shaping the way we communicate, entertain, and inform ourselves in our digital worlds.

Moreover, understanding AI helps demystify how it drives innovation. As AI technologies evolve, businesses leverage them to streamline operations, improve customer experiences, and foster creativity. AI's capacity for data analysis and predictive modeling allows companies to anticipate market trends, optimize supply chains, and make informed decisions, ultimately fostering growth and competitiveness.

The simulation of human intelligence doesn't end at professional applications. AI is deeply embedded in personal technology as well. Smartphones with voice recognition systems, smart home devices, and self-driving cars are tangible examples of AI impacting daily routines, illustrating how integral it has become in modern living.

However, comprehending AI also means addressing broader societal changes. Regulatory frameworks, such as GDPR, have been introduced to uphold privacy when processing personal data through AI systems. These measures ensure ethical practices in AI development and deployment, reinforcing the need for transparency and accountability when handling sensitive information.

As AI becomes pervasive, there's a critical need to balance technological advancement with ethical considerations. This involves not only protecting individual privacy but also ensuring AI systems are built responsibly and adapt to evolving regulatory standards. The necessity for adaptive systems reflects society's growing awareness of AI's potential implications, both positive and negative.

In education, AI offers considerable opportunities. It can personalize learning experiences for students by analyzing their strengths and weaknesses, fostering individualized teaching methods. Similarly, AI aids research by automating data analysis and offering insights that were once out of reach due to sheer volume or complexity.

With these points considered, AI's dual nature—as both a tool for augmentation and a subject for rigorous oversight—becomes clear. Its applications span beyond simple automation or efficiency gains and venture into areas like enhancing creativity, driving innovation, and redefining human-AI collaboration.

1.2 Types of AI

Artificial Intelligence (AI) is a rapidly evolving field with different types, each possessing unique characteristics and capabilities. Two major categories in AI are Narrow AI and General AI, both of which play significant roles in the development and application of intelligent systems.

Narrow AI, also known as Weak AI, is designed to perform specific tasks efficiently. It excels in areas where tasks can be clearly defined and automated, such as image recognition, speech processing, and recommendation systems. For instance, virtual assistants like Siri or Alexa use Narrow AI to process voice commands and provide accurate responses within their limited scope. Similarly, platforms like Netflix or Amazon employ recommendation algorithms to suggest content based on user data and preferences, showcasing how Narrow AI enhances user experiences by personalizing services.

The fundamental characteristic of Narrow AI is its specialization. Unlike humans, who can adapt to various environments and tasks, Narrow AI systems lack generalization capabilities. They are programmed to perform specific functions and cannot transfer their knowledge across different domains. This specialization allows them to outperform humans in particular tasks but confines them to predefined operational boundaries. For example, a facial recognition system powered by Narrow AI can identify individuals accurately in security contexts, yet it cannot reason beyond its programming to make sense of ambiguous images. Therefore, understanding the limitations of Narrow AI is essential to preventing unrealistic expectations regarding its capabilities.

On the other hand, General AI, or Strong AI, aims to mimic comprehensive human-like intelligence. The goal of General AI is to create machines that can understand, learn, and apply knowledge across diverse fields, similar to human cognition. While still a theoretical concept, General AI represents a significant leap forward in AI research and development. Unlike Narrow AI, General AI seeks to solve complex problems by reasoning through unfamiliar situations and adapting to new information as humans do.

Despite being in its nascent stages, the pursuit of General AI poses exciting possibilities and challenges. If achieved, General AI could revolutionize industries by providing advanced solutions to multifaceted problems. Fields like automated scientific research, where machines generate hypotheses and conduct experiments, could benefit immensely from General AI's cognitive abilities. However, developing General AI involves overcoming significant hurdles, such as ensuring safety, ethical considerations, and managing unintended consequences. These aspects must be addressed to harness General AI's full potential responsibly.

A crucial step in understanding AI technologies involves distinguishing between Narrow AI and General AI. Recognizing their differences helps clarify the current state of AI and its future trajectories. While Narrow AI operates within well-defined parameters, General AI aims to achieve a higher level of adaptability and decision-making. This distinction is vital for grasping how AI technologies influence everyday life and their potential to shape various sectors.

Grasping the nuances of AI types aids individuals in recognizing practical applications and limitations. The capabilities of Narrow AI have already made significant contributions to industries such as healthcare, where algorithms assist in diagnosing diseases and analyzing medical data rapidly and accurately. By alleviating repetitive tasks for healthcare professionals, these AI systems enable practitioners to focus on primary care, ultimately improving patient outcomes. In contrast, General AI, when fully realized, could transform these processes further by offering solutions that require higher-order reasoning and cognitive skills.

Understanding Narrow and General AI provides valuable insights into how AI technologies enhance business innovation. Business professionals can leverage AI-powered tools to optimize workflows, automate decision-making, and improve customer service. For example, implementing machine learning algorithms in supply chain management can enhance efficiency by predicting demand fluctuations and optimizing inventory levels. By embracing AI's capabilities, businesses can achieve greater productivity and maintain competitiveness in dynamic markets.

For entrepreneurs and freelancers, comprehending the distinctions between AI types empowers them to integrate AI into their ventures effectively. With an understanding of Narrow AI, they can utilize chatbots or automated marketing strategies to streamline operations and deliver personalized experiences to clients. Similarly, staying informed about advancements in General AI prepares them to explore new opportunities and align their businesses with emerging technological trends.

1.3 Common Misconceptions

In the realm of artificial intelligence (AI), myths abound, often fueled by rumors, popular culture portrayals, and sensationalist media. One of the most persistent myths is that AI will imminently take over the world, usurping human roles and rendering industries obsolete. Addressing these misconceptions is vital for fostering a rational and informed discourse about AI's actual capabilities and limitations.

Firstly, debunking the myth of AI domination helps alleviate unnecessary fear and panic. Popular culture has frequently depicted AI as an almost omnipotent force capable of outsmarting humans at every turn. Movies and books have portrayed AI as malevolent entities plotting to surpass human control, leading to widespread anxiety about technological advancement. However, these scenarios are largely fictional. Presently, AI is primarily designed to perform specific tasks rather than achieve autonomous consciousness or self-awareness. By clarifying AI's current scope and capabilities, we can reduce unfounded fears and encourage more grounded discussions about its role in society.

AI should be recognized as a tool rather than a sentient entity. This distinction promotes realistic expectations of its uses. Unlike science fiction narratives, modern AI does not possess desires, motivations, or emotions. Instead, it follows instructions based on algorithms and data input. Understanding this can shift perceptions from seeing AI as a threat to appreciating it as a valuable assistant augmenting human capabilities. By acknowledging AI's lack of autonomy, stakeholders can better harness its potential across various sectors without fearing unintended consequences.

Educating on AI's real capabilities versus futuristic myths supports informed discussions. Despite claims of AI possessing superintelligence, current technologies rely heavily on human oversight and guidance. Machine learning models, deep neural networks, and other AI forms require meticulous programming and constant updating to function correctly. They do not evolve independently beyond their programmed parameters.

Highlighting these realities equips audiences to discern be-tween hype and actual technological progress, enabling a more balanced dialogue about AI's implications.

Clarifying misconceptions encourages an open-minded per-spective among users and stakeholders. Accurate information dispels myths, allowing individuals to explore AI's benefits without being hampered by apprehension. For instance, rec-ognizing AI's utility in automating repetitive tasks can lead to improved efficiency and innovation within businesses. Rather than viewing AI with skepticism, organizations can embrace it as a means to elevate productivity and streamline operations. This open-mindedness is crucial for fostering collaborations between technologists, policymakers, and industry leaders to safely and effectively integrate AI into various fields.

A key guideline to consider when integrating AI applications is ethical deployment. While AI can greatly enhance business operations, maintaining transparency and fairness in its appli-cations ensures trustworthiness. Institutions should prioritize developing guidelines that safeguard against bias, privacy violations, and unjust outcomes. This ethical framework mitigates potential misuse while maximizing AI's societal benefits.

Furthermore, understanding AI's true nature can inspire cu-riosity and engagement with technology. Dispelling myths paves the way for educational initiatives that emphasize AI's transformative potential. Introducing AI concepts in schools and workplaces increases awareness and positions individuals to actively participate in shaping its future. Rather than

succumbing to fear, societies can channel energy toward exploring AI-driven innovations that address pressing challenges
like climate change, healthcare deficiencies, and economic
inequality.

Recognizing AI as a partner rather than a competitor redefines
our relationship with technology. It encourages collaboration
where humans and machines work symbiotically to achieve
common goals. By dispelling myths about AI domination, we
create opportunities for humans to focus on creative, strategic, and empathetic tasks that complement AI's data-driven
strengths. This approach emphasizes coexistence over competition, unlocking new possibilities for growth and development.

1.4 Real-World Examples

Artificial intelligence (AI) has gradually woven itself into the
fabric of our daily lives, often without us even realizing it. At its
core, AI is designed to mimic human-like decision-making and
learning abilities, making our everyday tasks more efficient
and intuitive. One of the most visible applications of AI in our
everyday routines is through voice recognition systems and
smart home devices. These technologies have moved beyond
mere novelty items and have become integral parts of modern
living.

Imagine waking up on a chilly morning and asking your digital
assistant to turn up the heat while you prepare for the day. This
seamless interaction is made possible by AI-powered voice
recognition systems that can understand, process, and execute
commands. Devices like Amazon Alexa, Google Assistant,

and Apple Siri rely on advanced algorithms to interpret your words and determine the action you want them to perform. Voice recognition technology is not only about understanding language but also understanding the context in which commands are given. For instance, when you ask an AI assistant to "switch off the lights," the system knows you're referring to the lighting in a specific room rather than all the lights in the house.

Smart home devices elevate this interaction further by connecting multiple gadgets under one ecosystem. For example, AI-enabled thermostats can learn your heating preferences over time, adjusting settings automatically to enhance comfort or efficiency. The integration of these devices fosters a connected environment where AI can optimize energy consumption based on your usage patterns. Smart soundbars, another application, adjust audio settings depending on whether you're watching a movie or listening to music, creating personalized experiences that align with your preferences.

These practical use cases help demystify AI, transforming abstract concepts into tools that simplify our routines. By interacting with AI in these straightforward ways, we begin to see its potential beyond basic automation. Recognizing AI's presence in our daily activities can spark curiosity about its broader implications. For instance, as we grow accustomed to AI managing our homes, we might start to wonder how it could revolutionize other aspects of life, such as health care, education, or transportation.

Moreover, contemplating AI's role in everyday life opens

doors to discussions about ethical considerations and future developments. As we interact with these technologies, we're encouraged to think critically about data privacy, the balance between convenience and security, and how AI might affect job markets and social structures.

More than just a convenience, AI serves as a bridge between theory and practice. By observing how it enhances our daily routines, we gain insights into the inner workings of AI systems. This understanding empowers us to make informed decisions about adopting new technologies and integrating them into our lives. For instance, knowing how AI processes information can influence our perception of its capabilities and limitations.

Furthermore, AI's incorporation into daily tasks provides tangible evidence of its effectiveness. It offers real-world examples that demonstrate the practical benefits of AI, such as improved efficiency, cost savings, and increased accessibility. These examples anchor theoretical knowledge, making it accessible to individuals without technical backgrounds. They show that AI is not restricted to complex scientific realms but is actively reshaping ordinary experiences.

As AI continues to evolve, its applications will extend even further into various domains. Imagine autonomous vehicles navigating city streets, predictive algorithms enhancing medical diagnoses, or personalized learning environments adapting to individual student needs. Each of these scenarios stems from foundational AI technologies already ingrained in our lives. Observing AI in mundane settings prepares us for these advanced implementations, helping us grasp the transformative power of AI across different sectors.

In essence, AI's presence in our daily tasks does more than just make life easier; it acts as an invitation to explore the fascinating world of artificial intelligence. By engaging with AI-driven technologies regularly, we develop an appreciation for their complexity while recognizing their profound impact on society. This awareness fosters a culture of innovation and curiosity, motivating people to embrace AI's possibilities in diverse fields, from business and education to entrepreneurship and beyond.

1.5 Difference between AI, Machine Learning, and Deep Learning

Artificial intelligence (AI) is a term that encompasses a wide array of technologies aiming to simulate human cognitive abilities in machines. At the heart of AI are two essential methodologies: machine learning and deep learning. Understanding these key components and their interrelationships is crucial for anyone venturing into the field of AI, whether as a beginner or an experienced professional.

First, let's explore the overarching nature of AI itself. AI serves as a broad umbrella under which various technological approaches can be found with the common goal of enhancing machine autonomy through improved learning and decision-making capabilities. Within this expansive domain, machine learning and deep learning play vital roles, acting as pillars that uphold the sophisticated structure of modern AI systems.

Machine learning is fundamentally about creating algorithms

that empower machines to learn from data, experiences, and past interactions without being explicitly programmed for each task. This ability to adapt and improve over time marks a significant advance from traditional computing methods. For instance, when you use a recommendation system on a streaming platform, it's employing machine learning to suggest content based on your previous viewing habits. The algorithm adapts, continuously refining its suggestions as it processes more data, illustrating how machine learning enables systems to evolve with minimal human intervention.

Diving deeper, we find ourselves in the realm of deep learning, which builds upon the principles of machine learning but distinguishes itself by utilizing artificial neural networks. These networks mirror the complexities of the human brain, making them adept at handling intricate tasks like image and voice recognition. Deep learning models require large amounts of data and substantial computational power, often necessitating specialized hardware, such as GPUs, to function effectively. A prime example of deep learning in action is in autonomous vehicles. The cars interpret sensory data from their surroundings to navigate safely, demonstrating the prowess of neural networks in processing massive datasets to make real-time decisions.

The distinction between machine learning and deep learning often comes down to data requirements and complexity. While machine learning can work effectively with smaller datasets and simpler correlations, deep learning thrives on extensive data, engaging in non-linear problem-solving that uncovers deeper insights. Consider facial recognition software used in security systems; it relies heavily on deep learning networks to accurately identify individuals even in varied lighting or angle conditions, showcasing how deep learning excels where precision and adaptation are critical.

Understanding these distinctions not only clarifies what each methodology entails but also enhances our comprehension of their specific roles and applications within the AI landscape. Machine learning often acts as the initial step in AI implementation, providing systems with the ability to improve over time using diverse inputs. From predictive analytics in business to personalized learning environments in education, the benefits of machine learning are vast and varied, directly impacting industries worldwide.

On the other hand, deep learning represents a more advanced stage, often implemented once foundational machine learning solutions have been established. Its capability to mimic human-like thinking makes it invaluable for tasks demanding high-level intuition and pattern recognition. For example, medical diagnostics systems employ deep learning to parse complex imagery and data, aiding doctors in identifying diseases with unprecedented accuracy and speed.

By demystifying these relationships, we can appreciate how machine learning and deep learning contribute uniquely to the grand design of AI, each serving specific functionalities that, together, drive innovation and efficiency across sectors. This understanding is pivotal, particularly for businesses looking to integrate AI technologies into their operations. By discerning the appropriate application of machine learning or deep learning, enterprises can optimize workflows, enhance customer experiences, and ultimately, fuel growth.

Moreover, for students and tech enthusiasts, grasping these concepts opens new avenues for exploration and potential career paths in technology. As AI continues to evolve, staying informed about these foundational elements ensures readiness to engage with emerging advancements and opportunities.

1.6 Final Insights

Throughout this chapter, we've delved into the fundamental concepts of artificial intelligence (AI) and its related fields. We've explored how AI aims to simulate human intelligence in machines, enabling them to learn from experience, adapt to new inputs, and perform tasks typically requiring human intellect. This exploration has highlighted the roles of machine learning and deep learning as key components driving AI's evolution. Machine learning empowers systems to enhance their performance over time, while deep learning, with its intricate neural networks, navigates complex challenges like image and voice recognition. These insights help demystify AI's presence in our lives, illustrating how it enhances daily interactions and optimizes various industries.

For those new to AI or looking to leverage its capabilities in business or personal projects, this chapter has offered a straightforward guide to understanding its foundational aspects. Recognizing the distinctions between Narrow AI, which handles specific tasks, and General AI, aspiring for broader cognitive abilities, broadens our appreciation for how

AI technologies shape our world. As AI continues to integrate into education, health care, and everyday devices, grasping these basics becomes increasingly important. Whether you're a student, a professional, or an entrepreneur, comprehending these principles equips you to navigate the evolving landscape of AI with confidence and curiosity.

Chapter 2: AI in Daily Life: Enhancing Everyday Experiences

Artificial Intelligence (AI) is seamlessly weaving itself into the fabric of our daily routines, offering enhancements that often go unnoticed yet profoundly impact our lives. From the moment we wake up to a room perfectly lit to our preferences, AI is at work, tailoring our environments to suit us. This chapter will delve into how AI technologies effortlessly become part of our everyday experiences, whether through smart home devices or intuitive voice controls, enriching our lives with convenience and efficiency.

In this chapter, you'll discover how AI operates behind the scenes in our homes, adjusting the ambiance with smart lighting systems that learn from our habits and surroundings. We'll explore the integration of voice-activated assistants, which make managing household tasks a breeze, as well as the personalized recommendations that streaming services provide based on our viewing history. By examining these various facets, you'll gain insight into how AI not only simplifies but also enhances our daily experiences, promising a future where technology anticipates our needs with minimal intervention.

2.1 AI in Home Devices

Smart Lights

Artificial intelligence (AI) has revolutionized the way we inter-act with our homes, making them smarter and more efficient. At the forefront of this transformation are smart lighting systems, which cleverly optimize energy usage by tailoring brightness to user habits and surrounding conditions. Imagine lights that intuitively know when to dim in the evening or brighten during an overcast day, seamlessly adapting to our needs without a thought on our part. These AI-driven systems conserve energy, thereby saving money, and contribute to a sustainable lifestyle by reducing unnecessary electricity consumption.

Beyond their energy-saving capabilities, these smart lights significantly enhance user comfort. By learning individual preferences and schedules, they automatically adjust to create the ideal lighting environment at any given time. For instance, if someone prefers a soft glow in the morning but vibrant light in the evening, the system adapts effortlessly. This reduces the need for manual adjustments, allowing individuals to focus on what truly matters throughout their day.

Integration with broader home automation systems further elevates the experience, enabling the creation of personalized environments tailored to one's lifestyle. The entire ecosystem of a home can work in harmony, where lighting, temperature, and even entertainment systems sync to suit personal moods or activities. Imagine preparing to wind down for the night;

with a simple command, the lights dim, the thermostat adjusts, and calming music begins to play—all without lifting a finger.

Voice-activated controls play a crucial role in this seamless integration, offering an easy and intuitive way to manage lighting. As technology becomes increasingly ingrained in our lives, the demand for convenience grows. Voice control meets this need by eliminating the physical interaction required to operate switches. Simply uttering a command like "turn off the lights" or "set the mood lighting" modifies the ambiance to your specifications instantly.

The accessibility of voice-activated controls also democratizes smart home technology, making it easier for everyone, including those with mobility challenges, to manage their living spaces with ease and independence. Interacting with home devices through natural language commands transforms the user experience into something more human-centered and less technical.

Smart Thermostats

AI is subtly yet significantly transforming the way we manage indoor climates, exemplified by its role in enhancing energy efficiency and user comfort within modern heating and cooling systems. At the heart of this innovation are smart thermostats, intelligent devices that possess the capability to learn and adapt over time. They evaluate diverse data inputs such as user preferences, historical temperature adjustments, and even external weather conditions, to automatically optimize temperature settings. This learning process not only creates an ideal environment for occupants but also minimizes energy consumption, offering a win-win scenario of comfort and cost savings.

By closely observing user behavior, AI-driven systems can create personalized thermal profiles for each household member. For instance, during winter, if a user consistently adjusts the thermostat to a particular setting at a specific time in the evening, the system will detect this pattern. As a result, it pre-emptively warms the home before the user's arrival, ensuring immediate comfort without the need for manual adjustment. Such dynamic adjustments help maintain cozy living spaces while actively reducing unnecessary use of heating or cooling resources.

The convenience of controlling one's home environment from anywhere in the world is another groundbreaking advantage introduced by AI through smart thermostats. Via smartphone applications, users can remotely manage their home's climate settings with remarkable ease. Picture this: you're returning from a lengthy trip on a scorching summer day. A few taps on your phone allow you to cool your living space before you step through the door. The ability to adjust settings remotely doesn't just mean greater convenience; it translates into tangible energy savings by preventing excessive use. No more forgetting to turn off the air conditioning when you're away or arriving home to a sweltering room.

Moreover, these systems utilize past data to generate comprehensive insights into a household's energy consumption patterns. Such analysis empowers users to make informed decisions about their usage. By understanding which times or settings demand more energy, homeowners can plan adjustments that balance comfort and cost-efficiency. These insights often reveal surprising patterns that could lead to further optimizations—perhaps discovering that lowering the overnight temperature slightly could result in significant monthly savings.

Crucially, the wider adoption of smart thermostats plays a pivotal role in advancing sustainable living. Energy conservation is no longer just a personal financial consideration but a collective environmental responsibility. By reducing superfluous energy expenditure, these devices contribute significantly to decreasing carbon footprints. For example, during periods of non-occupancy, such as vacations, the intelligent automation of temperature settings ensures minimal energy wastage without compromising future comfort upon return. The ecological impact may seem minor on an individual scale, but collectively, these efficient practices yield substantial environmental benefits, aligning personal convenience with global sustainability goals.

While traditional thermostats require users to manually set and adjust temperatures, AI-enabled versions eliminate this repetitive task. They're smart enough to sync with other home automation systems, creating seamless integrations where lights dim, curtains close, and the thermostat adjusts— all to suit your mood or schedule. This cohesive network simplifies daily routines and enhances overall quality of life. By automating mundane tasks, AI allows users to focus on more critical engagements, all while maintaining personalized comfort levels within their homes.

Looking to the future, the evolution of smart thermostats hints at even more sophisticated interactions. As AI technology advances, we anticipate further enhancements in their predictive capabilities, providing an even more nuanced approach to energy management. Imagine a system that not only responds to immediate changes in external temperatures but also predicts fluctuations days ahead using weather forecasts. Such foresight could optimize efficiency like never before, adjusting energy usage proactively to align with both current needs and anticipated circumstances.

Voice Assistants

AI Voice assistants have become indispensable tools in our daily lives, streamlining tasks and operations through sophisticated AI technology. With their advanced features, they are revolutionizing the way we interact with technology, allowing us to perform various activities hands-free and with ease.

Voice assistants like Amazon Alexa, Google Assistant, and Apple's Siri facilitate hands-free communication and information retrieval, significantly enhancing multitasking capabilities. Imagine a scenario where you're cooking dinner and suddenly need to set a timer. Instead of stopping what you're doing, you can simply ask your voice assistant to do it for you. According to a Statista survey, 27% of U.S. adults use voice assistants for hands-free navigation, highlighting the convenience and reliance on this feature. These assistants can also provide answers to questions, whether it's about the weather, sports scores, or even translating a phrase into another language. This seamless access to information without interrupting one's current activity liberates users from traditional device interactions.

The integration of voice assistants with smart home appliances extends their functionality beyond basic inquiries. Through simple voice commands, users can effortlessly control functions such as lighting and temperature. For instance, asking your voice assistant to dim the lights or adjust the thermostat can create a comfortable ambiance without needing to move from your spot. Smart home systems combined with voice technology allow for greater convenience, making everyday life more manageable. This capability not only enhances the user experience but also contributes to energy efficiency by ensuring that devices are used optimally and turned off when not needed.

Personalized user experiences are another critical aspect of how voice assistants streamline daily operations. With the ability to recognize individual voices and learning preferences over time, these assistants tailor responses and settings to suit personal tastes. Imagine being greeted with a customized news briefing relevant to your interests every morning, or having your playlist queued up based on your recent listening habits. Personalized interactions make everyday engagements more enjoyable and efficient. As they continually learn from each user interaction, voice assistants refine their responses and recommendations, offering an increasingly improved experience with each use.

In terms of task management, voice assistants prove to be invaluable. By setting verbal reminders, creating shopping lists, and organizing calendars, they help boost productivity and ensure that nothing slips through the cracks. Many people find juggling work, family, and social commitments challenging, but voice assistants simplify this by allowing users to verbally add events to their calendar or ask for reminders at specific times. Whether you're in the car and remember an important call you need to make or are preparing a grocery list while commuting, these assistants offer a convenient way to organize tasks without the need to manually enter data into a device.

Moreover, voice assistants support a growing ecosystem of third-party services that further expand their utility. They allow users to order groceries, book transportation, or even manage finances using just their voice. This level of integration promotes a smoother user experience across different aspects of daily life, eliminating the need to switch between multiple apps and interfaces. The flexibility offered by voice assistants, therefore, plays a crucial role in enhancing both personal and professional productivity, freeing up time for more meaningful tasks.

As AI voice assistants continue to evolve, they are expected to incorporate more advanced natural language processing capabilities, enabling them to handle even more complex tasks. The future holds promise for further personalization, context awareness, and integration with emerging technologies, which will only broaden their application scope. This trajectory indicates a continuous enhancement in how everyday tasks and operations are managed, ultimately improving individuals' quality of life in diverse ways.

2.2 Personalized Recommendations in Streaming Services

AI-driven recommendations significantly transform user experiences in both entertainment and shopping by offering tailored content that aligns with individual preferences. This personalization is made possible through the advanced algorithms employed by streaming services and e-commerce platforms, enhancing satisfaction and engagement for users.

Streaming services are a prime example of how AI can revolutionize live interactions by suggesting content based on individual viewing history and preferences. These services analyze user data, such as watch time and genre preference, to create profiles that guide content recommendations. The personalization provided improves viewer satisfaction since users discover films or series they are more likely to enjoy without spending time searching manually.

As algorithms continue to learn and adapt through repeated interactions, they become increasingly accurate. For instance, if a user frequently watches science fiction movies, the system will prioritize similar suggestions, enhancing the odds of finding appealing choices. This dynamic adaptability ensures that recommendations remain relevant and engaging, reflecting users' evolving tastes and preferences. By understanding patterns within user data, these systems can predict what content will likely appeal next.

The process of discovering new content becomes effortless due to the diverse offerings these recommendation systems provide. They expose users to a wider variety of genres and titles that they might not have encountered otherwise, contributing to an enriched entertainment experience. Viewers can easily explore different types of content, leading to higher engagement levels due to the novelty and diversity of options presented.

User engagement is also bolstered through a curated selection that sparks interest and encourages continual use. The assortment of recommended shows or products draws users back by consistently presenting exciting options. Streaming services focus on creating a captivating library of suggestions to keep audiences returning and exploring fresh content regularly.

In parallel, AI-driven recommendations in the shopping industry enhance consumer experiences by tailoring product suggestions to specific tastes. Similar to streaming services, online retailers utilize AI to analyze browsing habits, purchase histories, and even time spent considering particular items. This detailed analysis assists in crafting personalized shopping journeys where consumers are more likely to find items they want or need.

These recommendation systems do not merely rely on past behavior; they continuously update their suggestions in real-time based on current interactions. For example, if a shopper suddenly spends more time looking at fitness gear, the platform may promptly start showcasing related products. This level of real-time adaptation maintains relevance and interest, resulting in a more satisfying shopping excursion.

Additionally, these systems significantly simplify the search process, allowing customers to effortlessly locate desired products amid a vast array of options. As these systems streamline decision-making, shoppers recognize the value of convenience and efficiency, contributing to positive perceptions and increased usage.

Moreover, curated recommendations foster greater customer loyalty by offering consistently relevant suggestions and an enjoyable shopping experience. When consumers find value in their recommendations, they're likely to return, reducing the likelihood of switching to competitors. This loyalty helps businesses retain a committed customer base, ultimately enhancing brand success.

An important factor underpinning the efficacy of AI recommendations is trust. By integrating user feedback and reviews into the suggestion engine, AI can weigh these insights while generating new recommendations. Shoppers feel confident about their purchases when they consider others' experiences, thus increasing satisfaction and the likelihood of repurchase.

A striking example of this approach is Amazon's recommendation algorithm, which uses AI to drive personalized product suggestions. Their suggestions account for everything from previous purchases to browsing behaviors, ensuring that every user's home page feels individually designed. This personalized nature strongly impacts conversion rates, as customers often discover products they wouldn't actively seek out but are delighted to encounter.

2.3 E-commerce Platforms and Shopping

Personalized AI recommendations are shaping the future of online shopping by offering tailored experiences that resonate with individual consumers. At the heart of this transformation is the ability of AI to analyze users' browsing habits, enabling it to suggest products that align closely with their tastes and preferences. This not only enhances the efficiency of shopping but also elevates user satisfaction. By recognizing patterns in what consumers look at, add to their carts, or even purchase, AI can make informed predictions about other items they might be interested in. For example, if a customer frequently browses outdoor gear, AI may recommend complementary products such as hiking boots or backpacks. This level of personalization helps shoppers discover products more quickly, allowing for a seamless shopping experience.

Incorporating user reviews and ratings further refines these suggestions. AI systems can analyze feedback from thousands of users to determine product suitability and quality. When potential buyers see that recommendations are backed by positive reviews, trust naturally follows. For instance, if an item receives consistently high ratings across different aspects such as durability or value for money, customers are more likely to consider purchasing it. This integration of social proof into recommendations builds credibility, ensuring that users feel confident in their shopping decisions.

Moreover, AI plays a crucial role in tailoring marketing strategies, which leads to more relevant promotions and offers for consumers. By understanding customers' interests, shopping history, and demographic information, AI can craft marketing messages that resonate more personally. Gone are the days of generic advertisements; instead, customers receive targeted emails or notifications about sales on products they've shown interest in or new arrivals similar to past purchases. For example, if someone has recently bought yoga equipment, they might receive promotions for related items such as workout apparel or online yoga classes. These personalized marketing efforts not only boost customer engagement but also increase the likelihood of conversions, leading to higher sales for businesses.

Streamlining shopping processes through AI also significantly enhances consumer satisfaction. By automating routine tasks like product searches or even returns management, AI simplifies the overall marketplace experience. Not only does this make shopping more enjoyable, but it also saves customers time, enabling them to focus on discovering new products rather than getting bogged down by tedious processes. The introduction of AI chatbots is another way shopping is being streamlined. These virtual assistants provide instant support, answering queries related to product details, shipping information, or return policies. They ensure that help is available 24/7, thus reducing wait times and improving problem resolution. As AI learns from continued interactions, these chatbots become more adept at handling complex queries, thereby enhancing the overall user experience.

While these advancements offer numerous benefits, it's important for companies to follow best practices when implementing AI-driven recommendations. Transparency about data collection is crucial in building consumer trust. Customers should feel reassured knowing how their data is being used to enhance their shopping experiences. Additionally, testing and optimizing AI algorithms regularly ensures the effectiveness of product recommendations and marketing campaigns. Retailers must strive for a balance between personalized and general recommendations to avoid overwhelming shoppers while still encouraging discovery. Lastly, respecting customer preferences is paramount; providing users with the option to opt out of personalized recommendations if desired respects their autonomy and choices.

2.4 Final Insights

As we've explored, AI is reshaping the way we interact with our homes through seamless integration into everyday devices. From smart lights that adjust to our routines and preferences to thermostats that create comfortable environments while conserving energy, these technologies make life more convenient and sustainable. They not only simplify tasks like adjusting lighting and temperature but also provide personal comfort without any manual effort. This chapter highlighted how these smart systems work in harmony, providing a glimpse of what a connected home can achieve both in terms of ease and efficiency.

Looking forward, the potential for AI to further enhance our daily lives is immense. Whether it's through voice-activated controls that democratize technology or AI-driven personalized recommendations that enrich our entertainment and shopping experiences, these innovations illustrate the growing impact of AI in our routines. As this technology continues to evolve, it promises even greater integration and personalization, opening doors to new possibilities in how we manage our homes and activities. By understanding and embracing these changes, we are better equipped to leverage AI's benefits for improved living and environmental stewardship.

Chapter 3: AI and Transportation: Driving Innovation

Artificial intelligence is transforming the transportation sector. From self-driving cars to enhanced traffic management systems, AI technologies are becoming integral in redefining how we travel. This chapter delves into these innovations, exploring the intricate technologies that make it all possible. You'll learn about the sensors and algorithms empowering autonomous vehicles to navigate safely on their own, offering a glimpse into a world where human error is minimized, and road safety is significantly improved. This advancing technology promises not only convenience but also revolutionizes our daily commuting by potentially reducing traffic accidents and congestion.

As you journey through this chapter, you'll discover how AI is influencing various aspects of modern transportation. The chapter will cover the different levels of automation in vehicles, detailing the technological progress from basic driver assistance systems to the prospect of fully autonomous cars. Additionally, it discusses the rigorous testing and regulatory challenges these technologies face before they become a trusted reality on public roads. You'll also explore how AI enhances public transportation systems, optimizing routes and predicting maintenance needs to improve reliability and efficiency. Whether you're curious about the potential ethical implications or simply interested in understanding how these changes might affect personal travel experiences, this chapter offers insights into the fascinating intersections of AI and transportation.

3.1 Self-driving Cars and Their Technology

Self-driving cars, a marvel of modern AI technology, are not just concepts pulled from sci-fi fantasies but are becoming integral transitions in how we perceive travel. At the core of these autonomous vehicles lies an intricate array of technological advancements, each working harmoniously to revolutionize transportation. Central to this transformation are sensors, cameras, algorithms, and various sophisticated technologies that empower these vehicles to navigate autonomously.

One of the pivotal components in self-driving car technology is the use of sensors. These vehicles are equipped with a variety of sensors, including radar, ultrasonic sensors, and LiDAR systems. LiDAR, which stands for Light Detection and Ranging, plays a critical role by using lasers to measure distances between objects and create detailed 3D maps of the surroundings. This technology allows cars to detect obstructions, understand road contours, and adapt to real-time changes in their environment. Combining this with radar offers a reliable way to quickly detect moving or stationary objects, even in challenging weather conditions.

Complementing the sensor technologies, cameras serve as the eyes of these autonomous machines. Positioned around the vehicle, they gather visual data, capturing everything from lane markings and traffic signs to pedestrians and cyclists. Using computer vision, a branch of AI, these cameras analyze images in real-time, enabling the vehicle to recognize and classify different road elements accurately. This data becomes crucial in making split-second decisions necessary for safe navigation.

At the heart of decision-making in self-driving vehicles are powerful algorithms, often driven by machine learning techniques. These algorithms process the vast amount of data collected from sensors and cameras, allowing the vehicle to make informed decisions dynamically. For example, when approaching an intersection, the AI system evaluates various factors, such as the speed and trajectory of nearby vehicles, to determine the safest path forward. The continuous enhancement of these algorithms ensures that self-driving cars can handle complex driving scenarios with increasing precision and reliability.

One of the remarkable benefits of these technological advancements is their potential to significantly enhance road safety. Self-driving cars utilize predictive analytics to foresee possible collision scenarios and respond instantly. By constantly analyzing patterns and behaviors, the system anticipates potential threats from other road users and adjusts its actions preemptively. Immediate response capabilities, owing to rapid data processing, further contribute to avoiding accidents by reacting faster than a human driver could.

The promise of reduced traffic accidents is one of the most compelling arguments for the adoption of autonomous driving technologies. Human error accounts for a significant portion of road mishaps, and the integration of AI into driving aims to alleviate this challenge. With the ability to maintain precise control over acceleration, braking, and steering, autonomous vehicles minimize the common occurrences of rear-end collisions, lane drifting, and erratic driving behaviors that often lead to accidents. Moreover, the capacity to interconnect vehicles through advanced communication systems opens up possibilities for coordinated movement on roads, reducing congestion and the likelihood of collisions.

A step towards realizing these safety aspirations is already evident in current advanced driver assistance systems (ADAS) present in many modern vehicles. These systems serve as precursors to full autonomy, offering features such as adaptive cruise control, automatic emergency braking, and lane-keeping assistance. While these technologies still require a human driver's oversight, they underscore the incremental advancements leading towards fully autonomous systems.

Looking ahead, the implementation of self-driving vehicles promises to reshape urban landscapes and redefine personal commuting experiences. As companies continue to refine these technologies and address regulatory and ethical concerns, the societal acceptance and integration of autonomous vehicles appear increasingly promising. The gradual assurance through successful pilot programs and real-world testing will pave the way for these vehicles to become common fixtures in our daily lives.

3.2 Levels of Automation

From the hum of morning traffic to the rush of evening commutes, vehicles have always been closely tied to daily life. As technology advances, a new era in transportation unfolds with the rise of autonomous vehicles. Understanding different levels of driving automation is crucial for anyone interested in how self-driving technology evolves and integrates into society. This discussion details these levels, highlighting both the technological progression involved and the societal implications of each stage.

The Society of Automotive Engineers (SAE) developed a scale that outlines six levels of driving automation. These levels range from Level 0, or no automation, to Level 5, which represents full automation. Each level marks a significant step in self-driving technology, presenting unique challenges and opportunities. At Level 0, there is no automation whatsoever. Here, complete control lies with the human driver. The vehicle might include basic alert systems such as lane departure warnings, but these functions do not relieve any driving responsibilities from the person behind the wheel. This is what most drivers experience today; even though technology supports them in various ways, they remain in command of all driving tasks.

Moving up to Level 1, known as 'Driver Assistance,' we find the introduction of support features like adaptive cruise control or lane centering. While the technology assists with steering or acceleration and braking, it does so only one function at a time, requiring the driver to manage the rest. These systems help reduce driver workload but still demand constant attention.

Level 2 introduces 'Partial Driving Automation.' At this stage, the vehicle can control steering and speed simultaneously under limited conditions, thanks to advanced driver assistance systems (ADAS). Examples include Tesla's Autopilot and Ford's BlueCruise. However, drivers must keep their hands on the wheel and eyes on the road, ready to intervene as necessary.

Reaching Level 3 poses a greater leap forward, where 'Conditional Automation' allows the vehicle to handle all aspects of driving without driver oversight during certain scenarios, like highway cruising. Yet, drivers must be prepared to respond when the system requests intervention. Regulatory approval becomes more complex at this stage due to increased reliance on vehicle capabilities. For instance, Honda's Level 3 traffic jam assistance is legally approved only in Japan, illustrating the regulatory hurdles tied to such innovation.

Level 4, known as 'High Automation,' enables vehicles to operate independently within set parameters—think of pre-defined routes or specific geographic areas. These vehicles require no driver input except to set a destination. While close to full autonomy, their use is often confined to public transport services like driverless taxis and shuttles, where environmental controls are easier to maintain. This level suggests a future where public transport could operate more efficiently and cost-effectively, minimizing human error and increasing accessibility.

Finally, Level 5 brings us to 'Full Automation,' where vehicles perform all driving tasks under all conditions without human assistance. In this scenario, passengers are riders rather than drivers, free to focus on work, leisure, or relaxation. This level heralds a profound shift in how travel is perceived and experienced, yet widespread adoption faces obstacles. Technical advancements must ensure safety and reliability across diverse environments and weather conditions.

Understanding these levels provides insights beyond just technological feats; it also reflects the gradual integration of autonomy into society. Differing degrees of automation illustrate both progress in technology and the challenges of adoption. Level by level, they highlight how far we've come and where we're headed, from having the first ADAS systems to envisioning a fully autonomous vehicle ecosystem.

Adapting regulations and infrastructure to accommodate these changes remains an ongoing challenge. Authorities face the task of ensuring that new technologies coexist safely with traditional vehicles, necessitating updates to laws and driving norms. Public perception and acceptance also play a crucial role, emphasizing the need for transparency about the benefits and potential risks associated with autonomous vehicles.

This technological journey impacts various stakeholders, including automakers, regulators, and consumers. For automakers, it's a race to innovate. For regulators, it's about creating smart policies that protect public safety while fostering growth. Consumers must adapt to new ways of interacting with transport, redefining notions of privacy, convenience, and personal mobility.

Each level of automation offers a glimpse into future possibilities and probabilities. The distinction between these levels underscores not just technological prowess but societal readiness to embrace such profound change. As the world watches this evolution unfold, it's apparent that each step forward carries both excitement and apprehension, reflecting the dynamic interplay between innovation and societal adaptation.

3.3 Testing and Regulation of Self-driving Cars

Self-driving cars, a prominent example of AI's influence on transportation, are undergoing thorough testing to ensure they meet rigorous safety standards. The complexities of this process underscore the critical importance of adhering to these standards and complying with regulations, which have become focal points for industry stakeholders.

In the early stages of autonomous vehicle (AV) development, testing is conducted in controlled environments before these vehicles transition to real-world settings. This phased approach ensures that self-driving technology can address various challenges posed by different driving scenarios. Advanced driver assistance systems currently assist drivers in maintaining lane discipline or applying brakes automatically to prevent collisions. These features highlight how AI can dramatically reduce accidents caused by human error.

As exciting as this innovation is, it must navigate the regulatory landscape that governs its deployment. In the U.S., self-driving cars are subject to oversight by bodies like the National Highway Traffic Safety Administration (NHTSA) and state governments. However, there remains no specific regulatory requirement for companies to prove their vehicles' safety pre-implementation. Typically, regulations react after incidents occur, which has led to calls for more proactive measures. Achieving a balance between encouraging technological advancement and ensuring public safety presents ongoing challenges for policymakers, who must update frameworks and standards to keep pace with rapid developments.

Moreover, there is a significant public perception component tied to self-driving car regulations. The interaction between technological advancements and regulatory measures greatly impacts public confidence and acceptance of AVs. While the idea of autonomous vehicles promising safer roads is appealing, skepticism arises from high-profile accidents during testing phases. Ensuring transparency in testing results and regulatory decisions helps build trust among the general population, reassuring them that safety concerns are prioritized as much as innovation.

Safety protocols during testing are critical to preparing autonomous vehicles for societal deployment. Companies conduct exhaustive assessments to demonstrate compliance with Federal Motor Vehicle Safety Standards, ensuring vehicles operate without posing undue risk. This preparation extends to refining algorithms responsible for navigation and decision-making processes, accounting for unpredictable elements like pedestrians or adverse weather conditions. Testing also involves scrutinizing the vehicle's ability to handle emergency maneuvers, further removing the margin for errors attributable to human limitations.

As self-driving technology continues to evolve, industry players must harmonize efforts across development, regulation, and consumer outreach. Highlighting success stories where self-driving features prevent accidents serves as an example of potential safety improvements. By focusing resources on refining AI abilities to replicate — and ideally exceed — human decision-making skills, the industry could significantly lower current rates of traffic fatalities linked to human factors.

A comprehensive regulatory framework will include robust safety criteria, pre-market qualification tests, and transparent reporting of performance data. Regulators should encourage collaboration with tech developers to create standards based on empirical evidence and best practices. Policymakers need to anticipate future developments, establishing guidelines for when liability shifts from human drivers to automated systems — an area that remains inadequately addressed. Ensuring accountability through effective legal structures would bolster consumer confidence and catalyze wider adoption.

3.4 AI-Enhanced Traffic Management Systems

AI has become a transformative force in redefining traffic management systems, offering innovative solutions to enhance road safety and overall efficiency. Let's delve into the way AI is reshaping this field, making our travel experiences smoother and safer.

One of AI's significant contributions is its ability to optimize traffic signals through smart technologies. Traditional traffic lights often run on pre-set timers, but smart traffic signals powered by machine learning can adapt their timing based on real-time data. This approach allows traffic lights to adjust dynamically according to current traffic conditions. For instance, during peak hours, these systems can extend green light durations for congested lanes, thereby reducing waiting times and minimizing bottlenecks. Such real-time adaptability not only helps in easing traffic flow but also reduces vehicle emissions, promoting a more sustainable urban environment.

Beyond managing traffic signals, predictive traffic modeling is another area where AI demonstrates its prowess. By analyzing historical and real-time data, AI can anticipate congestion points and potential traffic snarls before they occur. This proactive management approach enables city planners and traffic authorities to implement preemptive measures such as altering traffic signal patterns or deploying traffic enforcers to critical areas, thereby averting potential gridlocks. Early identification of possible congestion points allows for effective planning and resource allocation, which in turn leads to enhanced commuter experiences and reduced travel times.

Incident detection is another crucial aspect where AI enhances traffic management. Real-time video surveillance combined with AI algorithms can quickly identify accidents or unexpected incidents on the roads. Once detected, AI can automatically notify relevant authorities and coordinate an immediate response. This swift action minimizes disruptions and ensures timely assistance, potentially saving lives. The rapid incident detection and response facilitated by AI expedite emergency services like ambulances and fire trucks, ensuring quick passage through traffic jams. Through intelligent traffic systems, municipalities can prioritize routes for emergency vehicles, improving overall public safety in crisis situations.

To make all these systems work seamlessly, effective data integration is vital. AI facilitates the integration of diverse traffic management systems into one cohesive unit, allowing for unified oversight. Different data sources, including GPS systems, video feeds, and weather forecasts, are harmonized to provide a comprehensive view of the entire traffic network. This harmonious integration supports a more coordinated traffic management strategy, enabling quicker decision-making based on accurate and updated information. Unified traffic oversight not only streamlines operations but also enhances the accuracy of traffic predictions and interventions.

It's important to note that while AI offers numerous benefits, there are several challenges and considerations that accompany its implementation in traffic management. Data acquisition, processing, and the need for robust cybersecurity measures are critical aspects that need addressing to ensure the reliability and efficacy of AI systems. Privacy concerns also arise regarding how personal information is used or shared, requiring transparent policies and communication to maintain public trust.

Despite these challenges, the economic advantages of utilizing AI in traffic management are compelling. Cost savings in time and fuel consumption, along with improved air quality from reduced emissions, present strong cases for cities looking to modernize their traffic infrastructure. Furthermore, optimizing traffic flow can lead to exponential improvements in daily life by empowering individuals to manage their time more efficiently, ultimately contributing to economic growth.

As we explore AI's transformative impact on traffic management, it's essential to keep in mind that human oversight remains integral. While AI can handle immediate issues such as traffic signal regulation and incident detection, strategic decisions related to long-term urban planning still require human judgment. The successful integration of AI in traffic management hinges on finding a balance between automation and human expertise to address both immediate and future transportation challenges effectively.

3.5 AI in Public Transportation Systems

The integration of AI into public transportation is transforming the way we experience and operate within these systems, bringing significant advancements in reliability, efficiency, and sustainability. Let's delve into how AI is making this revolution possible by examining the impact on route optimization, passenger experience, predictive maintenance, and sustainable transport solutions.

AI plays a pivotal role in optimizing public transportation routes, which leads to improved service reliability and greater commuter satisfaction. Using real-time data analysis, AI can scrutinize traffic patterns, road conditions, weather forecasts, and even historical commuting statistics to determine the most efficient routes for buses and trains. This level of optimization ensures that public transit services adhere closely to their schedules, reducing wait times and minimizing delays caused by unforeseen circumstances. Commuters benefit from knowing they can rely on accurate timetables, leading to a more seamless and satisfactory travel experience. According to reports, optimized routes not only save time but also reduce fuel consumption, contributing to operational efficiency.

Enhancing the passenger experience is another critical aspect where AI technology shines. By personalizing updates and notifications, AI significantly uplifts the overall user experience in public transport. With machine learning algorithms, AI can predict individual passenger needs and preferences, providing tailor-made travel suggestions or updates about delays, cancellations, and alternative routes directly to their smartphones. For instance, if there's a delay on a regular commuter's route, AI can suggest an alternate path, ensuring they reach their destination on time. This personalization fosters a sense of control and convenience for passengers, making public transportation more appealing compared to other modes of travel. Furthermore, AI can enhance comfort by adapting the climate control settings inside vehicles according to passenger preferences, creating a pleasant journey from start to finish.

Predictive maintenance is another game-changer in AI's application to public transportation. Traditional maintenance strategies often involve scheduled checks that can be inefficient and sometimes miss potential issues. With predictive maintenance, AI analyzes data from sensors placed on various components of vehicles, allowing it to detect early signs of wear and tear or malfunctions. By addressing these issues before they lead to breakdowns, AI minimizes service disruptions, resulting in fewer unexpected delays for commuters and reduced repair costs for service providers. It is estimated that predictive maintenance powered by AI can boost asset productivity by 20% and reduce overall maintenance expenses by 10%. This proactivity extends the lifespan of vehicles and infrastructure while maintaining consistent service quality.

AI also supports sustainable transport solutions through energy-efficient route management. By analyzing factors such as passenger load, vehicle capacity, and energy consumption, AI can devise routes that maximize fuel efficiency and minimize carbon emissions. These smart algorithms are essential for promoting eco-friendly practices in the transportation sector. AI not only guides route planning but also facilitates the integration of electric and hybrid vehicles into public transportation fleets. This transition further reduces the carbon footprint, aligning with global sustainability goals and fostering a greener urban environment. The role of AI in achieving sustainable transport cannot be overstated, as cities worldwide strive to lower emissions and enhance resource efficiency.

3.6 Final Insights

As we've explored in this chapter, AI is dramatically changing the way we travel. From the marvels of self-driving cars to the smart systems managing our traffic and public transportation, AI technologies offer innovative solutions that redefine our commuting experiences. Self-driving vehicles showcase an impressive blend of sensors, cameras, and algorithms, making them genuinely autonomous. These advanced technologies enhance road safety by reducing human error and prevent potential accidents through predictive analytics and rapid response capabilities. Furthermore, understanding the various levels of automation reveals how these innovations align with societal demands and regulatory frameworks.

Meanwhile, AI's role in traffic management and public transportation systems underscores its transformative impact on infrastructure and commuter satisfaction. Smart traffic signals adjust in real-time, optimizing flow and reducing congestion. In parallel, public transport systems leverage AI for better route management, personalized passenger experiences, and predictive maintenance, ensuring efficiency and reliability at every step. Together, these advancements not only promise a smoother travel experience but also point towards a future where technology and innovation pave the way for safer, more sustainable urban environments.

Chapter 4: AI in Healthcare: Revolutionizing Patient Care

A rtificial Intelligence is transforming healthcare by revolutionizing patient care through advancements in diagnostics and imaging. This chapter delves into how AI is changing the landscape of medical diagnostics, particularly its role in enhancing the accuracy and efficiency of analyzing medical images like X-rays, MRIs, and CT scans. As healthcare systems worldwide grapple with challenges such as human error and overloaded work schedules, AI emerges as a crucial ally for radiologists and other healthcare professionals. By providing rapid analysis and highlighting potential abnormalities that might be overlooked, AI tools help ensure better patient outcomes. The integration of technology in healthcare not only minimizes errors but also offers a fresh perspective on diagnosing diseases at earlier stages, which could significantly improve treatment success rates.

Furthermore, this chapter explores the growing use of AI in predictive analytics for patient care. It highlights how machine learning models use historical data to predict disease progression and optimize personalized treatment plans, thereby shifting the focus from reactive to proactive healthcare. Readers will learn about AI's impact beyond image interpretation, extending to electronic health records and report generation, which streamlines processes and allows healthcare professionals to dedicate more time to patient interaction. Additionally, the text addresses how AI-powered technologies contribute strategically to policy formulation and resource distribution within healthcare organizations. Through this examination, you'll discover how AI not only supports individual patient management but also fosters a broader understanding of population health trends—paving the way for innovative solutions in modern medicine.

4.1 AI in Diagnostics and Imaging

Artificial Intelligence (AI) is making significant advancements in healthcare, particularly in diagnosing medical conditions. One of the standout features of AI in modern medicine is its ability to rapidly and accurately analyze medical images. Technologies like computer algorithms can evaluate X-rays, MRIs, and CT scans with precision, assisting radiologists by identifying potential issues that might be missed or misinterpreted by the human eye, especially when fatigue or high workload is a factor.

Medical imaging errors can lead to misdiagnoses, which may negatively affect patient outcomes. AI significantly reduces these risks by minimizing human error. Algorithms trained on vast datasets accumulated from numerous scans provide consistent, reliable evaluations. These systems find subtle anomalies within images that can be indicators of early disease stages. By offering insights that may not be immediately

55

apparent to human observers, AI enhances diagnostic accuracy and ensures that potential health concerns are flagged for further examination.

Moreover, AI's capacity to predict disease presence using machine learning models is transforming diagnostics. This technology utilizes historical data, allowing it to identify patterns associated with specific diseases, such as rare genetic conditions or early signs of cancer. Through comprehensive data analysis, these models can foresee disease progression, potentially even before symptoms manifest physically. The foresight offered by AI aids doctors in developing preemptive treatment strategies tailored to individual patients, maximizing recovery chances and improving quality of life.

Beyond image interpretation, AI also streamlines the process of generating radiology reports. Typically, assembling these reports requires considerable time from radiologists, who must sift through large volumes of data. AI technologies expedite this process using natural language processing (NLP) to draft initial report structures, thereby reducing administrative burdens and allowing healthcare professionals to focus more on direct patient care and complex decision-making processes. Enhanced communication between healthcare providers facilitated by standardized AI-generated reports ensures that all parties involved have access to accurate and concise information, crucial for coordinated care efforts.

The integration of AI with Electronic Health Records (EHRs) further optimizes patient care by providing a holistic view of individual health profiles. For instance, linking AI tools with

EHRs enables the aggregation and analysis of diverse health data—from lab results to medication history— fostering a comprehensive understanding of patients' health over time. Such integrated systems support personalized treatment plans, adjusting medical approaches in response to new data while considering the patient's entire health history.

4.2 Predictive Analytics for Patient Care

The ability of AI to use data and predict patient health outcomes is transforming healthcare by enhancing care delivery. One of the primary uses of AI in this context is identifying patients at higher risk for complications, which enables proactive interventions. These predictive capabilities are driven by algorithms that analyze vast amounts of patient data. For example, by examining historical health records and current conditions, AI can forecast potential health issues before they become critical. This early detection allows healthcare providers to intervene quickly, potentially preventing emergencies and improving patient outcomes. Studies have shown that such predictive models are particularly beneficial for chronic diseases where early intervention can significantly alter the disease trajectory.

Moreover, AI's ability to evaluate large datasets plays a crucial role in identifying health trends. By analyzing patterns across diverse demographic groups, AI can guide resource allocation to areas most in need, ensuring that healthcare facilities are adequately prepared for anticipated demands. For instance, during flu season, AI models might predict an increase in respiratory-related illnesses, prompting hospitals to allocate more resources towards respiratory care units. This informed resource distribution not only enhances operational efficiency but also improves patient care quality, as facilities can provide timely and targeted treatments.

Another significant advancement is the integration of AI with wearable technology for continuous health monitoring. Wearables like smartwatches and fitness trackers collect real-time data on various health metrics, such as heart rate, activity levels, and sleep patterns. AI processes this data to offer personalized health insights and recommendations, empowering individuals to take charge of their own health. This continuous monitoring can alert users to potential health risks, encouraging preventive measures or medical consultations when necessary. The accessibility and convenience of wearables make them a valuable tool for managing personal health, particularly for individuals with ongoing medical conditions.

Complex decision-making in healthcare often places a heavy cognitive load on clinicians. Predictive analytics systems alleviate this burden by providing data-driven recommendations, allowing healthcare professionals to make informed decisions more efficiently. By presenting evidence-based treatment options and probable outcomes, these systems enhance the accuracy and speed of medical decisions. In critical situations, such prompt and precise recommendations can be lifesaving, ensuring that patients receive the best possible care based on comprehensive data analysis. For example, AI systems can suggest optimal drug dosages or alternative therapies based on individual patient profiles and historical treatment data, leading to more personalized care plans.

One key guideline to follow when implementing these AI technologies involves utilizing risk stratification models effectively. Risk stratification helps categorize patients according to their risk levels, enabling personalized care management approaches. Health practitioners should ensure that these models are regularly calibrated and validated to maintain accuracy and reliability. Through careful implementation and adjustment of these models, healthcare systems can improve their predictive accuracy and better serve patient needs.

4.3 AI-powered Wearable Health Tech

Artificial Intelligence (AI) is making significant strides in healthcare, particularly through its role in developing wearable health technologies. These wearables are revolutionizing how we monitor health, especially for chronic conditions. By continuously tracking vital signs, these devices help manage diseases like diabetes, cardiovascular illnesses, and respiratory problems more effectively. Their ability to provide real-time data ensures that both patients and healthcare providers can make informed decisions promptly, catching potential issues before they become serious complications.

One of the main functions of wearable health devices is to track vital signs such as heart rate, blood pressure, and oxygen levels. This continuous monitoring allows for a comprehensive evaluation of an individual's health, supporting the management of chronic diseases by providing essential data needed for timely interventions. For example, a person with hypertension can receive instant alerts if their blood pressure reaches concerning levels, prompting them to take immediate action or seek medical advice. This capability highlights the critical role wearables play in chronic disease management, offering both preventative and responsive benefits.

AI takes this process further by interpreting the vast amount of data collected by wearable devices. Through machine learning algorithms and data analysis, AI offers personalized feedback and recommendations to improve overall health outcomes. For instance, based on activity levels tracked by a smartwatch, AI can suggest alterations to exercise routines or dietary habits tailored to suit individual needs. By analyzing trends and patterns in the data, AI not only promotes healthier lifestyle choices but also anticipates potential health risks, thus enhancing preventive care measures.

In addition to personal health insights, these advancements foster improved communication between patients and health-care providers. Integrative health platforms serve as hubs that bring together diverse sets of health data into a cohesive overview. These platforms can integrate information from wearables with existing electronic health records, ensuring that doctors have a complete view of their patients' health history and current status. This integration enhances the dialogue between patients and providers, making consultations more effective and personalized since healthcare professionals can access detailed records at a glance, leading to more informed decision-making and personalized treatment plans.

The exploration of emerging AI technologies continues to push the boundaries of what wearable health technology can achieve. As AI algorithms become increasingly sophisticated, their predictive capabilities improve, allowing for more accurate tracking and management of chronic diseases. These advancements hold promise in enhancing the precision of health forecasts, which can predict flare-ups or other complications before they occur, thus paving the way for proactive healthcare solutions.

However, the rise of these technologies brings about ethical considerations that need careful address. Issues surrounding data privacy and security are paramount, as the sensitive health information collected by wearables must be protected against unauthorized access and breaches. Ensuring that data handling practices comply with regulations like the GDPR or HIPAA is crucial in maintaining user trust and maximizing the potential of these technologies in healthcare.

Moreover, the development and widespread adoption of AI-powered wearables face several challenges, including user compliance, cost, and accessibility. For these devices to reach their full potential, users must consistently engage with them, finding value in the data and insights provided. This requires devices to be user-friendly, comfortable, and seamlessly integrated into daily routines. Meanwhile, the high cost of advanced wearables and the infrastructures necessary for AI analysis can be prohibitive for some patients and healthcare systems. Efforts to address these barriers are essential to ensure that the benefits of wearable technology are accessible to all, regardless of socio-economic background.

Looking forward, future innovations in AI and wearable tech hold exciting possibilities. Enhancements in AI algorithms could significantly boost the accuracy and individualized nature of disease prediction and management. Additionally, integrating genomic data with real-time health data promises a new level of personalized medicine, potentially revolutionizing treatment strategies based on a person's genetic makeup. As battery efficiency improves, wearables will become more reliable and require less frequent charging, increasing their practicality for everyday use.

Expanding sensor capabilities further enriches the data wearables can provide. In the future, devices may measure additional physiological markers, such as hormone levels or even emotional states, offering a broader picture of one's health. Such insights could support more targeted interventions, improving the management of complex conditions and enhancing patient quality of life.

Finally, the integration of AI-enabled wearables with telehealth services can transform patient care delivery. By transmitting real-time data to healthcare providers remotely, wearables facilitate ongoing patient monitoring without the need for frequent clinic visits. This telehealth synergy is particularly beneficial for individuals living in remote areas or those with mobility challenges, ensuring they receive consistent care and attention despite geographical barriers.

4.4 Risk Stratification Models and Population Health Management

The integration of Artificial Intelligence (AI) into healthcare has sparked a revolution in understanding and managing population health trends. This transformative technology enables healthcare systems to analyze vast amounts of data, leading to improved decision-making and resource allocation. A significant aspect of this is the development of risk stratification models, which are crucial in identifying high-risk patients within a population.

Risk stratification refers to the process of categorizing patients based on their likelihood of developing health complications. These models allow healthcare providers to focus resources more effectively, ensuring that high-risk individuals receive the attention and care they need. For example, hospitals can use AI algorithms to analyze patient records, lifestyle factors, and genetic information to identify which patients might require intensive monitoring or interventions. This targeted approach not only improves individual health outcomes but also enhances the overall efficiency of healthcare services by reducing unnecessary treatments and hospital admissions.

Moreover, AI plays an instrumental role in public health strategies by analyzing large datasets. These datasets often include information from electronic health records, socio-economic data, and other sources that were previously underutilized due to their complexity. AI's ability to process and find patterns in these diverse data sources helps policymakers understand disease prevalence, predict outbreaks, and plan strategic healthcare interventions. For instance, during the COVID-19 pandemic, AI was used to track virus spread and evaluate the effectiveness of public health measures, aiding authorities in making informed decisions swiftly.

Supporting preventive care initiatives is another area where AI makes a substantial contribution by identifying community health needs. AI tools can mine data to determine which neighborhoods or demographic groups might be more susceptible to certain diseases due to environmental or behavioral factors. With this information, health organizations can implement tailored health education programs, vaccination drives, or screening tests specifically targeted to the communities most at risk. This proactive approach in addressing public health issues results in reduced healthcare costs and improved quality of life for individuals.

Tailoring treatment plans based on individual risk levels is yet another benefit facilitated by AI. In traditional healthcare models, treatment approaches were often generalized due to the lack of individualized data. AI allows for a shift towards personalized healthcare, wherein treatments are adjusted according to a patient's unique profile—considering factors such as genetics, environment, and lifestyle. By utilizing AI-driven insights, clinicians can offer treatment options that are more effective and have fewer side effects, directly enhancing patient safety and care efficiency. This precision medicine approach not only optimizes therapeutic benefits but also empowers patients to take control of their health, knowing that their treatment plans are customized for their specific needs.

Furthermore, AI's contributions to patient safety cannot be understated. AI-driven tools predict potential adverse events and readmissions, allowing healthcare professionals to preemptively intervene. For instance, machine learning algorithms can analyze post-discharge patient data to flag those at high risk of complications. Such predictive analytics guide timely follow-up actions, reducing readmission rates and ensuring continuous patient care outside hospital settings. This closed-loop healthcare system embodies the future of patient-centric care, where prevention and early intervention are emphasized over treatment.

Despite its numerous advantages, the integration of AI in healthcare does not come without challenges. Issues related to data privacy, algorithm bias, and the digital divide must be addressed to ensure equitable access and application of AI technologies across all populations. Ethical considerations regarding data use and transparency remain vital as we increasingly rely on AI-driven recommendations for managing population health.

Nevertheless, the future of AI in healthcare holds promise. As AI systems evolve, their capability to assimilate unstructured data alongside structured data will enhance their utility in comprehensive healthcare delivery. Collaboration between technology developers and healthcare providers is essential for continuous improvement and innovation. Engaging diverse stakeholders, including patients, in the development process ensures that AI tools are user-friendly, culturally sensitive, and aligned with public health goals.

4.5 Clinical Decision Support Systems

Harnessing the power of artificial intelligence (AI) in health-care is like unlocking a new realm of possibilities that can vastly improve patient care. A key area where AI has proven transformative is in empowering clinical decision-making processes, fundamentally altering how healthcare professionals approach diagnostics and treatment.

One of the most compelling aspects of AI is its ability to employ predictive analytics, enabling healthcare practitioners to make informed decisions promptly. This capability stems from analyzing vast amounts of data, identifying patterns, and predicting outcomes with remarkable precision. Predictive analytics draws on a wide range of data sources, including electronic health records (EHRs), imaging, and even genetic information, to forecast potential health issues before they become critical. By anticipating patient needs early, clinicians can intervene proactively, substantially reducing the risk of complications and improving overall patient care.

AI's prowess in reducing clinicians' cognitive load cannot be overstated. With evidence-based treatment protocol recommendations readily available, practitioners can focus more on patient interaction rather than wading through copious amounts of medical literature. This streamlining of processes ensures that clinicians have access to the latest evidence-based insights, enhancing their capacity to deliver top-tier medical interventions. For instance, AI algorithms can quickly compare a patient's current condition against thousands of similar cases, offering recommendation protocols that have been optimized for success.

Moreover, integrating AI into the workflow significantly improves patient outcomes, particularly in managing complex cases that require nuanced and timely interventions. Consider scenarios involving patients with multiple chronic conditions or those with rapidly evolving diseases—AI systems provide real-time updates and suggestions, allowing healthcare providers to adjust treatment plans dynamically. This responsiveness not only prevents deterioration of the patient's health but also facilitates optimal recovery trajectories by aligning treatments with best practices derived from global datasets.

AI also plays a crucial role in upholding adherence to best practices in healthcare settings. By embedding AI insights into daily operations, healthcare institutions can ensure consistency in patient care while minimizing human error. The integration of AI serves as a continuous feedback loop, educating healthcare teams on the efficacy of their choices and highlighting areas for improvement. It creates an environment where learning and adaptation are constant, leading to a culture of continuous improvement and excellence.

The impact of AI extends beyond individual patient interactions, influencing broader systemic changes within healthcare organizations. By providing robust data-driven insights, AI helps shape policies and operational strategies that prioritize efficiency and effectiveness. This fosters a holistic approach to healthcare delivery, where decisions are both patient-centered and informed by the latest technological advancements. As

AI continues to evolve, its application will likely expand further, offering increasingly personalized care while addressing diverse patient needs.

Despite these advantages, it is essential to acknowledge that the successful implementation of AI in healthcare hinges on careful consideration of ethical implications. Issues such as data privacy, algorithmic bias, and accountability must be diligently managed to ensure that AI enhances, rather than detracts from, patient care. Healthcare providers must engage in ongoing dialogue about the responsible use of AI, emphasizing transparency and trust with patients. Continuous monitoring and validation of AI models are vital to upholding safety and effectiveness standards.

4.6 Final Insights

As we've explored, AI's role in modern healthcare is transformative, particularly in diagnostics and imaging. By efficiently analyzing medical data, AI technology supports radiologists in detecting diseases early, thus minimizing human errors that could lead to misdiagnoses. The integration of AI with Electronic Health Records (EHRs) continues to enhance personalized patient care, using comprehensive health profiles for better treatment plans. Additionally, AI streamlines processes, allowing healthcare professionals more time for patient interaction by reducing administrative workloads. This thoughtful application of AI optimizes the healthcare ecosystem, ultimately improving diagnostic accuracy and resource management.

Furthermore, the predictive capabilities of AI significantly impact patient care by foreseeing potential health issues through data analysis. Wearable health tech has emerged as a game-changer, offering real-time health insights and empowering individuals to manage their well-being actively. Its integration with AI holds promise in making healthcare more accessible and efficient, especially with enhanced disease prediction abilities. Despite the ethical considerations regarding data privacy, AI-driven innovations continue to push boundaries, fostering an environment where proactive solutions are prioritized over reactive healthcare measures. The ongoing evolution of AI presents exciting opportunities for transforming how we understand and address health challenges in the future.

Chapter 5: AI in Business: Fueling Growth and Efficiency

A I is transforming the way businesses operate, particularly in enhancing growth and efficiency. As organizations face increasing demands to stay competitive, artificial intelligence offers innovative solutions to streamline processes and optimize resources. AI's influence extends across industries, prompting businesses to rethink their strategies and adapt to this new technological landscape. By leveraging AI, companies are not just keeping pace with change but are also setting themselves apart in the market. This chapter delves into how AI is not merely an optional tool but a vital instrument for modern business success.

In this chapter, you will explore the multifaceted role of AI in transforming business operations. It explains how AI is revolutionizing customer service through chatbots and virtual assistants, offering immediate and efficient support. Discover how data analysis powered by AI enables companies to make informed decisions quickly, enhancing strategic planning and execution. The chapter further examines AI's ability to automate repetitive tasks, freeing up human resources for more complex and creative endeavors. Finally, it highlights how integrating AI with business systems boosts operational efficiency, allowing seamless information flow and improving real-time decision-making capabilities. Through understanding these applications, readers will gain insights into harnessing AI's full potential for driving growth and achieving higher efficiency in their business environments.

5.1 AI in Customer Service: Chatbots and Virtual Assistants

In today's fast-paced digital world, businesses are constantly seeking innovative ways to enhance customer service. Artificial intelligence (AI) has emerged as a game-changing technology, revolutionizing how companies interact with their customers. One of the most prominent applications of AI in customer service is the use of chatbots, which provide instant, 24/7 support. These automated agents handle routine inquiries efficiently, allowing human staff to focus on more complex tasks. By doing so, businesses not only improve response times but also significantly reduce operational costs.

Chatbots are designed to offer real-time assistance to customer inquiries, ensuring immediate support without needing human intervention. According to Rafalski, chatbots' ability to work round-the-clock means that customers can always access help, even during non-business hours or holidays. This constant availability plays a crucial role in improving customer satisfaction by swiftly resolving routine queries, leading to quick resolution and positive experiences.

Moreover, AI-powered virtual assistants further enhance efficiency by automating repetitive tasks. These intelligent systems can manage various customer interactions, such as answering frequently asked questions and guiding users through processes. Virtual assistants optimize workflows by freeing up employees to tackle more intricate issues, thereby minimizing human error and boosting overall productivity. As reported by Globe, the implementation of AI tools like virtual assistants significantly enhances user experience and reduces bounce rates.

One key advantage of AI-driven customer service solutions is their seamless integration with Customer Relationship Management (CRM) systems. This integration enables businesses to access valuable customer data effortlessly, which in turn allows them to craft personalized strategies. The ability to retrieve information such as past interactions, purchase history, and preferences empowers companies to deliver tailored responses, fostering a deeper connection with customers. AI-based tools analyze customer information in real-time, providing insights that inform strategic decisions and enhance service delivery.

Furthermore, the use of natural language processing (NLP) capabilities within chatbots allows for more nuanced and personalized conversations. These advanced systems can understand human language, including sentiment and intent, enabling them to provide contextually relevant responses. This level of personalization not only makes interactions feel more human but also increases engagement and loyalty. As cited by HootSuite, conversational AI tools maintain context within a conversation, ensuring continuity and relevance in customer interactions.

The impact of AI on customer service extends beyond mere efficiency; it significantly boosts customer engagement and loyalty. By offering personalized experiences, AI-driven tools create meaningful connections with customers. For example, dynamic content generation allows chatbots to send tailored product recommendations and personalized offers based on individual preferences. This customization fosters a sense of appreciation among customers, making them more likely to return and remain loyal to the brand.

Cost-effectiveness is another compelling reason businesses are embracing AI in customer service. Automating repetitive and time-consuming tasks results in significant cost savings. According to Rafalski, industries worldwide are estimated to save over $2 billion in customer service costs by the end of 2024 due to AI-powered systems. These savings stem from reduced staffing requirements and increased efficiency, allowing companies to allocate resources more strategically.

Additionally, conversational AI tools facilitate multilingual support, enabling businesses to communicate with a diverse global audience. With language recognition and translation capabilities, chatbots can engage customers in their preferred languages, breaking down communication barriers and providing a seamless support experience worldwide. This feature is particularly valuable for businesses looking to expand their reach and cater to an international clientele.

Improved data collection is yet another benefit of AI-powered customer service solutions. Chatbots gather valuable information on customer inquiries, preferences, and behavior, offering insights that inform business strategies. By analyzing and recording interactions, companies can identify trends, patterns, and customer needs, ultimately leading to informed decision-making and enhanced customer engagement.

As businesses increasingly recognize the advantages of AI in customer service, they also appreciate its role in improving brand image. By adopting modern and innovative customer service solutions, companies demonstrate their commitment to staying current with industry trends. Conversational AI reflects a forward-thinking approach, positioning businesses as customer-centric and innovative. This perception strengthens the brand's reputation, attracting more customers and fostering trust.

5.2 AI-Driven Data Analysis for Decision Making

In today's rapidly evolving business landscape, artificial intelligence (AI) is playing a transformative role by accelerating data analysis and empowering strategic decision-making. AI's ability to process vast amounts of data in real-time ensures that businesses are not just reacting to changes but are proactively steering their operations toward more efficient outcomes.

Imagine a scenario where a company's sales team needs to make decisions about marketing campaigns instantly. With traditional methods, the team would need to analyze heaps of data manually, a process that could take days or even weeks. However, AI-driven analysis systems can sift through large data sets almost instantaneously, providing actionable insights right at the moment they are needed. This capability allows businesses to make prompt decisions based on current insights, keeping them ahead of market curves.

Predictive analytics, another powerful AI feature, helps businesses identify potential future trends by examining past and present data. For example, retail companies leverage predictive models to forecast which products will be in demand in upcoming seasons, allowing them to optimize inventory and supply chains. Such foresight offers a significant competitive advantage, as companies can prepare for trends before they fully materialize, thus meeting consumer demands more efficiently and effectively.

Moreover, one of the challenges businesses face when handling big data is transforming complex datasets into understandable formats. Here, AI-driven visualizations come into play. Tools like Tableau and Microsoft Power BI utilize AI to convert intricate datasets into charts, graphs, and dashboards that are easy to interpret. This simplification enhances understanding and facilitates communication across teams, ensuring everyone from executives to frontline employees can make informed decisions based on clear, succinct data representations.

An essential aspect of AI in business is its democratization of data. Previously, data analysis was the domain of technical experts, often leaving non-technical staff on the sidelines. Today's AI tools are designed with user-friendly interfaces that allow even those without a technical background to engage deeply with data. This accessibility fosters a data-driven culture within organizations, encouraging informed collaboration across departments. Employees can independently explore data insights, engage in meaningful discussions, and contribute to evidence-based decision-making processes.

For instance, let's consider a company utilizing an AI dashboard. A marketing manager without a data science degree can use these tools to analyze customer behavior patterns and adjust strategies accordingly. This empowerment bridges the gap between technical and non-technical staff, promoting a sense of inclusivity and shared purpose in achieving business goals.

The benefits of AI in data analysis extend beyond internal operations to customer interactions. By analyzing client data, AI systems can personalize customer experiences, suggesting products or services tailored to individual preferences. This customization not only enhances customer satisfaction but also builds long-term loyalty, a critical factor in sustaining business growth.

However, while AI offers substantial advantages, it's important for businesses to address some inherent challenges. The effectiveness of AI systems heavily relies on the quality of input data. Poor data quality can lead to inaccurate analyses and misguided decisions. Therefore, businesses must ensure their data is accurate, complete, and consistent. Additionally, as AI systems make autonomous decisions, ethical considerations regarding data privacy and algorithmic bias must be carefully managed.

Ultimately, the integration of AI in business operations, particularly in data analysis and decision-making, marks a significant leap forward in how organizations function. By adopting AI technologies, businesses can expect to see improved efficiency, enhanced strategic planning, and sustained competitive advantage. As AI continues to advance, its role in shaping intelligent business ecosystems will undoubtedly expand, ushering in an era of unprecedented innovation and productivity.

5.3 Automating Repetitive Tasks in Business Processes

In today's rapidly evolving business landscape, organizations are increasingly turning to AI automation as a key strategy for optimizing workflow efficiency and reducing operational costs. By automating routine tasks, businesses can reallocate valuable human resources to strategic roles, thereby boosting productivity and cutting expenses. This approach not only enhances the efficiency of daily operations but also positions companies to better adapt to market changes and demands.

Routine task automation is a pivotal component in this transformation, as it frees employees from mundane, repetitive tasks, allowing them to focus on more creative and strategic functions that drive business growth. For instance, consider an employee who originally spent significant time entering data into spreadsheets or manually processing information. With automation tools, these tasks can be completed with minimal human intervention, enabling employees to concentrate on decision-making processes, innovative projects, and customer interactions that add substantial value to the organization.

Robotic Process Automation (RPA) is a specialized technology within AI that has proven particularly effective in managing data entry and processing. RPA can execute thousands of transactions per second, handling huge volumes of data with precision and speed that surpasses human capability. The benefits are twofold: not only does RPA increase the speed and accuracy of data management, but it also significantly reduces the likelihood of human error. This reduction in errors leads to improved data integrity and reliability, which are crucial for making informed business decisions.

For example, in financial institutions where accuracy is paramount, RPA can streamline tasks such as loan processing, account reconciliation, and report generation. By automating these processes, banks can ensure accuracy and compliance, thus enhancing both customer satisfaction and regulatory adherence. The overall effect is a more streamlined operation that minimizes delays and maximizes resource allocation.

Furthermore, the integration of AI technologies within existing systems plays a critical role in ensuring smooth workflow operations and quick adaptability to change. AI solutions can seamlessly integrate with legacy systems, bolster functionalities, and promote interoperability across various departments. This integration ensures that data flows efficiently between systems, eliminating bottlenecks and facilitating real-time decision-making. As a result, businesses can respond swiftly to market fluctuations, customer demands, and emerging trends, maintaining a competitive edge in their respective industries.

A practical illustration of AI integration can be seen in supply chain management. Advanced AI algorithms can predict demand patterns based on past data and market indicators, allowing companies to adjust inventory levels accordingly. This proactive approach helps prevent overstocking or stockouts, thereby optimizing inventory costs and improving customer satisfaction through timely deliveries.

Beyond immediate efficiencies, AI automation also yields long-term savings by minimizing errors and maintaining consistent productivity levels. Reduced error rates mean fewer resources are allocated to rectifying mistakes, leading to significant cost savings over time. Moreover, AI systems operate around the clock without fatigue, ensuring continuous productivity and throughput. This level of consistency is invaluable, especially in manufacturing settings, where downtime can lead to substantial financial losses.

The implementation of AI-driven automation often requires an initial investment and planning phase. However, the return on investment (ROI) is typically realized quickly through reduced operational costs and enhanced efficiency. Businesses may start by introducing pilot programs to validate the effectiveness of automation strategies, gathering feedback, and refining processes based on real-world usage. This phased approach ensures that the transition to automated systems is smooth and well-received by employees, reducing any resistance to change.

It is essential for organizations embarking on this journey to invest in training and upskilling their workforce. Employees must understand how to work alongside AI tools effectively and adapt to their new roles within a digitally transformed environment. Comprehensive training programs that cover the fundamentals of AI, process automation, and human-robot collaboration are key to empowering employees and maximizing the benefits of automation.

Moreover, to sustain the advantages of AI automation, organizations should establish robust governance and monitoring practices. Defining clear roles, responsibilities, and performance metrics ensures accountability and facilitates ongoing improvements. Regular monitoring and reporting allow businesses to identify areas for further optimization and track the success of their automation initiatives.

5.4 Impact of AI on Customer Satisfaction and Retention

In today's fast-paced business world, artificial intelligence (AI) is making waves in enhancing customer relations and retention strategies. By utilizing AI solutions, companies can significantly increase engagement with their customers, thereby fostering loyalty through constant interaction. AI-driven tools such as chatbots, personalized communication systems, and automated responses ensure that businesses maintain an ongoing dialogue with their clientele. These interactions are crucial for understanding consumer needs, preferences, and grievances, which ultimately leads to improved satisfaction and loyalty.

One remarkable feature of AI is its ability to seamlessly gather and analyze vast amounts of data. Businesses can leverage

AI metrics to monitor customer satisfaction levels accurately. AI tools track customer interactions, feedback, and behavior patterns, enabling organizations to assess where they stand in terms of customer contentment. For instance, sentiment analysis, a technique powered by AI, helps companies gauge public opinion through social media posts, reviews, and other online content. By systematically evaluating this data, businesses can identify potential areas of improvement and implement necessary changes to enhance the overall customer experience.

The power of AI extends to developing efficient retention strategies. By proactively addressing user needs, companies can prevent churn and secure a loyal customer base. Predictive analytics, a branch of AI, plays a pivotal role here. These analytics allow businesses to predict future consumer behavior based on historical data. Such predictions help in anticipating customer demands and dissatisfaction before they surface, enabling timely interventions. For example, if AI models detect a decrease in brand interaction from certain customers, companies can deploy specific targeted campaigns to re-engage them.

Personalized experiences are increasingly becoming the cornerstone of effective customer retention, and AI facilitates these experiences at scale. Consumers today expect bespoke interactions that cater specifically to their needs and preferences. With AI, businesses can create customized messages, offers, and product recommendations tailored to each customer's unique profile. This level of personalization not only enhances the shopping experience but also strengthens the emotional connection between the consumer and the brand.

Consequently, it leads to higher rates of return customers, as individuals perceive value in continuing their relationship with the company.

Consider the example of eCommerce platforms using AI for recommending products. By analyzing past purchase history and browsing behaviors, AI can suggest items that a particular customer is more likely to purchase. This targeted approach boosts sales and reinforces customer bonds. When consumers feel understood and valued, they are more inclined to remain loyal to a brand. Moreover, because AI operates continuously, this personalized service can be maintained without significant human intervention, ensuring consistent quality of interaction.

Engagement doesn't stop at personalized recommendations; real-time interaction facilitated by AI is equally vital. For instance, AI-powered chatbots and virtual assistants offer immediate, round-the-clock support, ensuring customers receive help whenever needed. This accessibility reduces the frustration often associated with delayed responses, thus contributing to a positive customer perception. Chatbots can handle routine inquiries or escalate complex issues to human agents when necessary, maintaining a seamless service delivery that keeps customers satisfied.

Furthermore, AI allows real-time feedback collection and analysis, which is critical for continuous improvement in customer relations. Automated systems can sift through and analyze feedback from various channels almost instantaneously. Businesses can adjust their strategies accordingly, addressing any emerging concerns and continually refining their approaches to meet evolving customer expectations. This dynamic adaptability ensures long-term growth and sustenance in competitive markets.

A key benefit of incorporating AI into customer retention strategies is the automation of workflows. AI's efficiency in processing data, segmenting customers, and executing marketing campaigns autonomously saves time and resources. For example, AI can automatically send out personalized emails or notifications at optimal times based on individual customer habits, ensuring communication remains relevant and effective. This automation lets the marketing team focus on strategic tasks rather than get bogged down by repetitive processes, facilitating smoother operations and increased productivity.

Businesses must remember, though, that technology should complement, not replace, human interaction in customer service. While AI brings numerous advantages, it is important to strike a balance where technology supports human efforts in building personal relationships with customers. Training staff to effectively use AI tools ensures that the human touch in service is preserved, offering customers the best of both worlds—efficient technology paired with empathetic human care.

Adopting AI comes with a learning curve, especially for beginners or non-technical professionals. However, the potential payoff makes it a worthwhile investment. Companies should aim to keep their teams updated on the latest AI trends and tools, encouraging a culture of learning and adaptation. This preparation will empower employees to maximize AI capabilities, driving better customer engagement and retention outcomes.

In conclusion, AI plays a fundamental role in transforming how businesses interact with their customers. From increasing engagement and satisfaction levels to crafting proactive retention strategies, AI equips companies with the tools needed to nurture lasting customer relationships. As industries continue to evolve, embracing AI's full potential will undoubtedly be a defining factor in achieving sustained success in customer relations.

5.5 Integration of AI with Business Systems

In today's evolving business landscape, the seamless integration of AI into existing business infrastructures is not just an aspiration but a necessity. AI enhances software functionalities, streamlining departmental operations and fostering unified workflows. This integration allows companies to overcome traditional operational hurdles and creates more efficient ways of working collaboratively across departments.

At the heart of this transformation is AI's capability to improve and automate software processes. By doing so, it significantly reduces the complexity often found in traditional software systems. For instance, outdated systems may require separate inputs from multiple sources, leading to data silos and inefficiencies. AI resolves these issues by integrating disparate data streams, providing a cohesive platform that centralizes and harmonizes information flow throughout an organization.

Furthermore, as businesses face dynamic market conditions, adaptability becomes crucial. AI-enhanced systems enable organizations to react swiftly to changes in the business environment. This agility is vital in maintaining competitiveness, enabling businesses to pivot or adjust strategies quickly based on real-time insights. For example, AI-driven predictive analytics can foresee market trends, allowing businesses to align their resources and strategies effectively.

The advantage of AI in providing real-time data accessibility cannot be overstated. Real-time access ensures that teams are informed and equipped to make faster decisions. In scenarios where time-sensitive decisions are required, such as supply chain management or customer service interactions, having immediate access to current data through AI tools enables teams to respond promptly and appropriately. This enhanced capability leads to increased trust in the data being used and elevates the quality of decision-making within the organization.

Moreover, the seamless integration of AI tools facilitates smoother transitions when implementing new processes or technologies. As businesses expand or shift their focus, transitioning without disruption is key to maintaining momentum and avoiding costly downtime. AI provides a robust framework that supports these transitions by ensuring the continuity of workflows and enhancing the utility of existing tools. The interconnectedness fostered by AI also means that any updates or enhancements to one part of the system are automatically mirrored across other dependent operations, minimizing lag time and errors.

Consider a situation where a company is rolling out a new product line. AI's cohesive integration capabilities allow for a smooth introduction of new components with minimal disruption to ongoing business activities. The connected systems facilitated by AI ensure all parts of the operation—from production to logistics—are aligned and functioning optimally. This integrated approach maximizes resource use and ensures that each department works in sync towards shared organizational goals.

While the benefits of AI integration are clear, it's important to acknowledge that transitioning to AI-enhanced systems may present initial challenges. Companies need to invest in training and development to equip their workforce with the necessary skills to leverage these technologies fully. However, the potential gains, including reduced operational costs, improved productivity, and enhanced workflow efficiency, outweigh the temporary challenges associated with implementation.

As AI continues to evolve, its potential applications in business will only grow. Organizations must remain open to embracing these technologies and exploring innovative uses across various sectors. The future of business lies in leveraging AI not just as a tool for efficiency but as a catalyst for innovation and growth. By actively seeking out opportunities to incorporate AI into their infrastructure, businesses position themselves at the forefront of technological advancement, ready to capitalize on new developments as they arise.

5.6 Final Insights

In this chapter, we've explored how artificial intelligence is transforming customer service and business operations, focusing on the roles of chatbots and virtual assistants. By integrating AI tools like these, businesses can enhance efficiency and customer satisfaction, providing 24/7 support and freeing staff to tackle more complex challenges. These AI-driven tools improve response times, cut operational costs, and enable personalized interactions that build stronger customer relationships. For businesses, it's not just about adopting new technologies but understanding how these tools can streamline processes and create meaningful experiences for customers.

For beginners or business professionals, adopting AI solutions doesn't have to be intimidating. The key takeaway is that AI offers practical benefits, from automating routine tasks to analyzing customer data for better decision-making. By leveraging AI, companies can become more agile, make informed decisions, and ultimately deliver superior service. As AI continues to evolve, its potential to reshape industries will only grow, offering exciting opportunities for those willing to embrace this technological shift. Whether you're a student, entrepreneur, or tech enthusiast, understanding AI's impact on business operations opens up a world of possibilities for innovation and growth.

Chapter 6: Education and AI: Shaping Future Learning

E ducation and artificial intelligence, once distinct realms, are now intertwined in shaping the future of learning. AI's potential to transform educational experiences is vast, from adapting teaching methods to suit individual needs to introducing new ways to engage with content. This chapter invites you to explore these possibilities, unveiling how AI's integration into education fosters an environment where students can thrive. By tailoring learning experiences to individual students, AI enhances engagement and caters to various learning styles, which are pivotal for student success.

Throughout this chapter, you'll delve into how personalized learning systems utilize AI to revolutionize traditional approaches, offering insights into adaptive learning technologies that assess student performance and adjust curricula accordingly. You will discover how data-driven tools provide real-time feedback, enabling educators to make informed decisions about instruction strategies. Additionally, the chapter highlights how gamification techniques and AI-driven content creation contribute to keeping educational material relevant and captivating. As AI continues to evolve, it holds the promise of delivering customized educational pathways, enhancing student engagement, and ultimately leading to improved academic outcomes.

6.1 Personalized Learning Systems

In today's rapidly evolving educational landscape, personalized learning systems are becoming essential tools in tailoring educational experiences to meet the diverse needs of students. By leveraging adaptive learning technologies, personalized approaches not only increase engagement but also support various learning styles, ultimately enhancing educational outcomes.

Adaptive learning technologies serve as a cornerstone in personalizing education. These technologies analyze student performance through sophisticated algorithms, assessing how each student interacts with content and identifying areas where they excel or struggle. For instance, when a student consistently performs well in mathematics yet encounters difficulties in science, the system can adjust the curriculum to reinforce scientific concepts while maintaining a steady pace in math. This customization ensures that students remain engaged by interacting with material that is challenging but attainable, preventing frustration or disengagement.

The power of adaptive learning lies in its ability to create personalized learning paths. Unlike traditional educational models that apply a one-size-fits-all approach, personalized learning allows students to progress at their own pace. This flexibility caters to individual differences in learning speed and style, accommodating those who may need more time on specific subjects and offering advanced materials to others ready for faster progression. By allowing students the freedom to move forward once they have mastered a concept, this method enhances retention rates and ensures a deeper understanding of the subject matter.

Data-driven insights play a crucial role in refining these personalized experiences. Through continuous collection and analysis of data points such as quiz scores, assignment completion times, and interaction patterns, educators receive real-time feedback about student progress. This wealth of information empowers teachers to make informed decisions, enabling them to tailor instruction strategies that address unique student needs immediately. Real-time feedback fosters an environment where both students and educators can engage in meaningful dialogue about progress, challenges, and goals, making learning a collaborative process.

Moreover, gamification techniques significantly boost motivation and engagement in learning environments. By incorporating game mechanics like rewards, levels, and leaderboards into educational settings, these systems transform routine learning activities into interactive and enjoyable experiences. For example, a history lesson could become a quest where students earn badges for completing tasks or answering questions correctly. Gamification taps into intrinsic motivations such as competition, achievement, and curiosity, creating a compelling educational atmosphere that encourages students to persist even when faced with challenges.

Integrating AI with gamification further personalizes these experiences, adapting the difficulty of tasks based on individual progress. If a student breezes through initial challenges, the system can introduce more complex problems to maintain their interest. Conversely, if a student struggles, it can simplify concepts or provide hints to aid comprehension. This adaptability keeps learners in their zone of proximal development, maximizing educational benefits without overwhelming them.

As technology advances, AI-driven content creation promises even greater customization of learning materials. AI can generate personalized educational content tailored to different learning preferences, ensuring all students find resources that resonate with them. Whether it involves adjusting reading materials to suit more visual learners or providing auditory options for those who benefit from listening, AI tailors educational experiences to maximize effectiveness.

Furthermore, as learning analytics tools become more sophisticated, they offer valuable guidelines for optimizing educational outcomes. By analyzing extensive datasets, these tools identify patterns and trends in student performance, facilitating interventions for those who might be falling behind. Educators can then implement targeted support strategies, such as additional practice sessions or personalized tutoring, to bridge any gaps. This proactive approach ensures that all students receive the assistance they need to succeed, contributing to higher overall academic achievements.

Incorporating AI-driven content creation into educational curricula enhances these systems' capabilities. By automatically updating materials according to current trends, AI ensures that content remains relevant and engaging for students. Additionally, it allows for quick adaptation of resources to accommodate varying skill levels and interests, offering a customized educational experience that aligns more closely with individual learner profiles.

6.2 AI Tutors and Educational Bots

In today's rapidly evolving educational landscape, AI tutors and bots have emerged as powerful tools, reshaping the way learners receive individualized support. These virtual counterparts offer a unique advantage—consistent availability for continuous learning. Unlike traditional settings where instructors may be constrained by time and availability, AI-powered virtual tutors provide one-on-one assistance anytime a student needs it. This constant accessibility ensures that learning is not interrupted, allowing students to reinforce concepts, practice skills, and clarify doubts at their own pace.

Virtual tutors excel in offering personalized, interactive support. Imagine a student struggling with a complex mathematical concept; an AI tutor can guide them through each step of the problem-solving process, adapting its explanations to match the student's understanding level. This tailored approach makes learning more efficient and effective, catering to the diverse needs of individual students. The adaptability of AI tutors stands out in contrast to the one-size-fits-all model of traditional education, paving the way for a more inclusive and engaging learning environment.

Alongside AI tutors, chatbots have gained prominence in educational settings, providing immediate responses to student inquiries. This functionality enhances support systems by addressing questions in real-time and significantly reducing the workload on educators. For instance, instead of waiting hours or even days for a teacher's email response, students can interact with a chatbot to get instant clarifications on topics they find challenging. This immediacy not only aids students but also allows educators to focus on more complex instructional duties rather than spending considerable time on basic queries.

Furthermore, chatbots contribute to creating a supportive atmosphere where students feel encouraged to ask questions without fear of judgment, thus promoting active participation and deeper engagement with course material. To effectively maximize these benefits, educational institutions should guide students on how to leverage chatbots optimally, ensuring they enhance rather than detract from critical thinking skills. Implementing clear guidelines on when and how to use chatbots can ensure that these tools supplement learning without fostering dependency.

AI-driven assessment tools bring another dimension to personalized education by evaluating student performance intricately. These tools analyze various aspects of a learner's capabilities, offering personalized feedback that highlights strengths and areas needing improvement. For example, language learners benefiting from AI assessments can receive detailed insights into their grammar usage, vocabulary range, and pronunciation accuracy, which helps direct their study efforts more efficiently.

Moreover, AI-enabled practice quizzes and simulations provide ongoing opportunities for self-assessment, encouraging students to track their progress over time. By doing so, learners can take ownership of their educational journey, identifying topics requiring additional focus—an approach that promotes a proactive learning attitude. It's essential for educators to incorporate structured guidelines on utilizing AI assessments responsibly to maintain academic integrity and prevent misuse.

Mentoring systems represent yet another facet of AI's role in education, connecting students with mentors who guide them in career pathways and networking opportunities. These systems harness AI algorithms to match students with mentors based on interests, aspirations, and fields of study, fostering meaningful connections that might otherwise remain unexplored.

The value of mentorship has long been recognized in education and professional development. With AI-enhanced matching systems, students are empowered to engage in dialogues with industry professionals, gaining insights that formal education alone might not provide. Such interactions can be instrumental in shaping career decisions and expanding networks, proving beneficial for future employment prospects.

Guidelines here can help students understand the importance of building relationships with mentors while avoiding over-reliance on automated systems. Encouraging mentees to actively participate in discussions, prepare thoughtful questions, and seek continuous growth ensures that mentoring remains an enriching bilateral experience.

As we advance further into the digital age, the integration of AI tutors and bots in education will undoubtedly become even more sophisticated. Their potential to transform the learning experience is immense, offering tailored educational experiences that adapt to the unique needs and preferences of every student. However, it is crucial to balance technological integration with the invaluable human elements that nurture holistic development and lifelong learning habits.

6.3 AI in Academic Research and Data Analysis

In an educational landscape increasingly shaped by digital innovation, AI tools have emerged as pivotal assets in streamlining academic research and enhancing data analysis workflows. These tools utilize advanced algorithms to automate complex tasks, thus saving time and enabling a deeper focus on critical thinking and creativity.

AI-assisted research tools significantly enhance the efficiency of literature reviews. Traditionally, researchers spent extensive hours sifting through countless papers to identify relevant studies, a process that was both time-consuming and prone to human error. With the advent of AI, tools like Litmaps provide automated literature review capabilities. They can prioritize studies based on citation patterns and relevance scores, thereby dramatically reducing the time required for compiling comprehensive reviews. This automation frees researchers to dedicate more energy toward interpreting findings and developing innovative hypotheses rather than getting bogged down in preliminary data gathering.

Alongside literature reviews, data mining techniques play a crucial role in identifying trends and patterns within educational data. Educational institutions generate vast amounts of data, ranging from student performance metrics to administrative records. AI algorithms can sift through this data to detect meaningful patterns that inform strategy and decision-making. For instance, data mining can uncover correlations between teaching methods and student outcomes, guiding schools in adopting best practices that enhance learning experiences. Moreover, these insights are increasingly used to tailor educational content and methodologies to better suit varied learner profiles, further optimizing educational strategies.

Data mining techniques benefit from a structured approach, including identifying objectives, preparing data, selecting appropriate mining algorithms, evaluating patterns, and implementing results. By adhering to these steps, educational institutions can harness AI's full potential, leading to insights that drive strategic decisions.

Predictive analytics is another groundbreaking application of AI in education. By analyzing historical and real-time data, these systems can forecast student performance with remarkable accuracy. For educators, this means they can identify students who may be at risk of underperforming well before their grades begin to slip. This predictive insight allows schools to implement targeted interventions—such as tutoring programs, personalized learning plans, or additional resources—ensuring that students receive the support they need to succeed. The ability to anticipate challenges and address them proactively exemplifies how AI not only enhances educational outcomes but also fosters a more inclusive learning environment where every student's potential can be realized.

Collaboration platforms enhanced by AI are revolutionizing how research is conducted across institutions. Traditionally, collaboration was hampered by geographical constraints and the inherent difficulty of synchronizing efforts across different locations. AI-powered platforms obliterate these barriers by providing seamless, cloud-based environments where researchers can share data, ideas, and findings in real-time, regardless of where they are situated. Tools that facilitate this kind of connectivity allow for greater access to diverse expertise and perspectives, enriching the research process and accelerating discovery. For instance, AI-driven collaboration tools can recommend potential collaborators based on shared research interests or citation networks, paving the way for more strategic and impactful partnerships.

These advancements promote a more interconnected academic community, breaking down silos and fostering a culture of open knowledge exchange. As researchers collaborate across disciplines and borders, AI becomes a catalyst for interdisciplinary innovation, which is essential for addressing today's complex educational and societal challenges.

6.4 AI-driven Content Creation

Artificial Intelligence (AI) is transforming the educational landscape by enabling the creation of personalized educational materials. This approach allows educational content to be tailored specifically to meet different learning needs, preferences, and styles, ensuring that every student receives an engaging and relevant learning experience.

One way AI achieves this personalization is through custom content generation. AI can analyze data from students' interactions, including their strengths, weaknesses, and preferred learning modalities. By doing so, it creates content that aligns with a student's unique learning style, thereby enhancing both engagement and comprehension. For instance, visual learners might receive more diagrammatic representations of information, whereas auditory learners might be provided with podcasts or spoken word videos. This level of customization helps in maintaining the material's relevance, making the learning process not only more effective but also more enjoyable for students.

Moreover, automated development of educational materials means that educators can save significant time on preparing content, which can then be dedicated to direct student interaction and support. Traditionally, teachers spend a considerable amount of time creating lesson plans, quizzes, and other instructional materials. With AI-driven tools, much of this workload is reduced as these systems can generate tests, assignments, and even lecture notes based on up-to-date curriculum data. This automation allows educators to focus on what truly matters—spending quality time nurturing students' understanding and actively engaging with them in the classroom.

Staying current with educational trends is another advantage of AI-generated content. As knowledge evolves rapidly in various fields, AI algorithms continuously update educational materials to ensure alignment with the latest standards and developments. For example, in subjects like computer science or environmental studies, where new discoveries and technologies emerge frequently, AI can swiftly incorporate this fresh information into teaching resources. This capability not only keeps the curriculum relevant but also helps students stay informed about contemporary issues and innovations that shape their field of study.

Additionally, AI tools provide the flexibility needed to quickly adapt educational materials to accommodate diverse skill levels and interests within a single classroom. In traditional settings, teaching a heterogeneous group often poses challenges, as students have varying degrees of prior knowledge and interests. AI addresses this challenge by dynamically adjusting learning resources and pathways. For instance, if a student shows proficiency in a particular topic, AI can introduce more advanced resources to keep them challenged. Conversely, if a student struggles, the system can recommend remedial exercises or simplified explanations, thus providing a tailored learning journey for each individual.

Personalized recommendations are crucial in helping students discover educational resources that match their specific needs.

By leveraging sophisticated algorithms, AI can suggest books, articles, videos, and other digital content based on a student's past performance, interests, and goals. Such personalized recommendations enhance the learning experience by enabling students to delve deeper into areas they find intriguing, thereby fostering a sense of autonomy and motivation in their educational pursuits.

Furthermore, AI systems offer real-time feedback, which is vital for continuous improvement in education. Through features like automated grading and immediate response to student queries, learners receive prompt insights into their progress. This timely feedback loop empowers students to address gaps in understanding promptly and encourages steady advancement toward their learning objectives.

Importantly, while AI significantly aids in personalizing education, human teachers remain indispensable. The synergy between AI tools and educators ensures a balanced approach where technology handles routine tasks, and teachers focus on creative and critical aspects of instruction. Educators play a crucial role in interpreting AI-derived insights to inform strategic decisions that optimize their teaching methods, providing the empathetic support and inspiration essential for nurturing well-rounded learners.

6.5 Learning Analytics Tools

In modern classrooms, the integration of artificial intelligence (AI) in educational tools has revolutionized the way student progress and performance are monitored. This transformation hinges on the capabilities of AI to collect, analyze, and utilize data to provide a comprehensive understanding of each student's learning journey. By analyzing this data, educators can make more informed decisions to enhance teaching strategies and outcomes.

AI-driven progress monitoring tools facilitate targeted interventions for students who may be struggling, thereby significantly enhancing their learning outcomes. In a study conducted with a group of 100 gifted and talented students from 3rd to 6th grade, it was shown that those who were in classrooms equipped with progress monitoring technology performed better in post-tests compared to those taught using traditional methods. This remarkable improvement is largely attributed to the immediate feedback provided by these tools, which allows students to learn at their own pace. For teachers, it simplifies the process of adjusting instruction to match the skill levels of individual students, effectively differentiating instruction and preventing them from falling behind.

Moreover, AI tools offer educators comprehensive data that augment their decision-making processes, potentially leading to improved teaching strategies. Such data not only highlight areas where students excel or struggle but also reveal patterns in learning. With this information, educators can refine their lesson plans and instructional methods to address the unique needs of each class. Strategies like Response to Intervention (RTI) and Positive Behavioral Interventions and Supports (PBIS) are examples of approaches where progress monitoring plays a crucial role in making informed adjustments to teaching methodologies.

Identifying learning patterns through AI is another critical advantage. By continuously collecting and evaluating data points, educators can identify trends in student behavior and learning preferences. This capability allows for the development of better curriculum design and instruction methods that cater to diverse learners. Progress monitoring data serve as a guide to adapt teaching materials and approaches, ensuring they are relevant and effective for a broad spectrum of students.

Furthermore, AI enables real-time tracking of student engagement, allowing for timely support and adjustments. As noted in research, when educators follow data in real time, they can modify lesson plans or instruction to better suit students' needs. This proactive approach ensures that students remain engaged and motivated, as they receive the necessary support exactly when they need it. By comparing students' rate of improvement against set goals, educators can assess whether current methods are effective or if additional interventions are required.

In practice, schools implementing AI-driven monitoring tools find themselves equipped with the means to tailor educational experiences to the individual student. This personalization is particularly beneficial for special education settings, where students often present varied learning abilities and challenges. Progress monitoring can be customized to track specific skills and competencies, allowing for detailed insights into each student's progress. The flexibility of these tools in adapting to different subjects and learning styles makes them invaluable in both general and special education environments.

To ensure the effectiveness of progress monitoring tools, educators must adhere to established guidelines and maintain fidelity in the administration process. This involves regular training for staff to ensure they understand the purpose and implementation of progress monitoring. Additionally, developing clear plans for data collection and analysis helps avoid inconsistencies that could affect the accuracy of the insights gained.

6.6 Final Insights

In this chapter, we've journeyed into the world of AI-enhanced learning systems, discovering how they transform educational experiences by tailoring them to individual needs. Personalized learning systems use adaptive technologies to customize education based on each student's unique learning pace and style. This approach contrasts sharply with traditional models, offering a more engaging and effective way for students to learn. These systems don't just adapt content—they also leverage real-time data to empower educators, providing insights that help refine teaching strategies. As a result, AI allows for a more dynamic and supportive educational environment, aligning learning materials and methods closely with student preferences and performance patterns.

Moreover, integrating AI into learning doesn't stop at personalization; it extends into motivation and accessibility. By incorporating gamification techniques, AI makes learning interactive and enjoyable, encouraging students to stay engaged even when faced with challenges. The use of chatbots and virtual tutors ensures constant support, allowing students to receive help whenever needed, fostering a sense of autonomy in their educational journey. Whether you're a beginner aiming to understand AI's basics or a professional seeking ways to enhance your work through innovation, these advancements highlight how AI can revolutionize education. They promise a future where learning is continuously adapted to meet individual needs, paving the way for more inclusive and effective educational landscapes.

Chapter 7: AI in Entertainment: Crafting New Experiences

Artificial intelligence (AI) has become a captivating element in the entertainment industry, redefining how content is crafted and offered to audiences. This chapter delves into AI's transformative power in gaming, illustrating its role in reshaping virtual worlds through ground-breaking techniques like procedural generation and intelligent non-playable character development. Such innovations are not just enhancing gameplay but also unlocking new realms of creativity that were once thought unreachable. By automating intricate processes and personalizing player experiences, AI is democratizing game design, making it more accessible and inclusive for developers and gamers alike.

As we journey through this chapter, readers will discover the multifaceted applications of AI across different entertainment platforms beyond gaming. From revolutionizing movie pro-duction through advanced scriptwriting analytics to pioneering new frontiers in music and art creation, AI is a formidable tool in the creative arsenal. We'll also explore how AI optimizes content distribution, engages diverse audiences, and even aids in real-time narrative adjustments, crafting personalized user experiences that set the stage for future entertainment possibilities. Emphasizing AI's dual role as both a collaborator and an innovator, this chapter invites readers to envision a future where technology and creativity intersect to expand what's possible in storytelling and audience engagement.

7.1 AI in Gaming Innovations

In recent years, artificial intelligence (AI) has emerged as a transformative force in the world of game development, significantly altering how games are created and experienced. One of the most notable advancements driven by AI is procedural generation, which allows developers to create expansive and dynamically generated worlds. Through procedural generation, algorithms can design intricate landscapes, cities, or entire universes, providing players with endless opportunities for exploration. This technique not only saves countless hours of manual labor but also enables developers to focus more on crafting immersive narratives and unique gameplay experiences. Games such as "Minecraft" and "No Man's Sky" exemplify this, offering vast, procedurally generated environments where each player's journey is distinct and ever-changing.

Another innovative application of AI in gaming involves the development of intelligent non-playable characters (NPCs). Traditionally, NPCs followed scripted behaviors, often leading to predictable and repetitive interactions. However, AI has infused these characters with new life by allowing them to adapt and respond to players in real-time. By employing behavior trees and machine learning algorithms, NPCs can now exhibit personalities, evolve their strategies, and interact with the game world in complex ways. For instance, in "The Elder Scrolls V: Skyrim," NPCs follow daily routines that make the world feel organic and alive, resulting in more engaging narratives and increased replayability. As AI technology continues to evolve, we can expect even richer storylines and deeper player engagement.

Enhanced game analytics represent another frontier where AI significantly impacts player experience. By analyzing player data, including preferences, play styles, and interaction patterns, AI-driven analytics tools provide insights that enable game developers to refine mechanics and personalize content. This process helps predict points where players might lose interest, allowing developers to intervene proactively with updates or new features that foster retention and enhance enjoyment. Game analytics not only benefit developers in optimizing their creations but also empower players with experiences tailored to their unique tastes. In this context, guidelines around how to implement and utilize game analytics effectively are crucial. Developers should focus on creating transparent policies regarding data collection and ensuring player privacy, fostering trust between players and creators.

AI's influence extends even further into virtual reality (VR), where it plays a pivotal role in personalizing interactive environments and advancing new storytelling genres. In VR settings, AI can adjust narrative elements and environmental features based on player actions, enabling deeply immersive experiences that feel intuitive and responsive. For instance, AI systems might modify the difficulty level of a VR game in real-time by monitoring physiological indicators such as heart rate or player gaze, ensuring an engaging yet tailored adventure. Additionally, VR storytelling benefits from AI's capacity to integrate multiple narrative paths, allowing players to shape their own stories within highly interactive and dynamic realms.

As we explore these advancements, it's essential to consider how AI technologies are seamlessly blending into various facets of game development. While procedural generation, intelligent NPCs, enhanced game analytics, and VR personalization highlight specific areas of impact, the overarching theme is AI's ability to democratize and elevate the creative process. This democratization empowers both industry professionals and aspiring game designers by reducing entry barriers and expanding access to powerful development tools.

Moreover, the collaborative nature of AI ensures ongoing innovation as developers continually experiment with new applications and methodologies. By embracing AI-driven technologies, the gaming industry not only enhances existing formats but also paves the way for entirely new genres and experiences. From adaptive narratives that change based on player choices to virtual realms that offer limitless exploration, AI is redefining what is possible in gaming, making it more immersive, inclusive, and engaging than ever before.

7.2 AI in Movie Production and Editing

In today's rapidly evolving film industry, AI has emerged as a transformative force, streamlining filmmaking processes and enhancing the overall cinematic quality. One of the primary areas where AI is making a significant impact is script and story development. By analyzing popular trends and audience preferences, AI provides filmmakers with insights that can inform more strategic filmmaking decisions. This data-driven approach empowers writers and producers to craft stories that resonate well with audiences, thereby increasing the likelihood of box office success. For instance, AI algorithms can analyze the components of blockbuster films, such as character arcs and plot twists, and suggest similar elements for new scripts. This predictive capability enables studios to produce content that aligns with current market demands and audience expectations.

Moreover, the automation of editing tasks through AI technologies is revolutionizing the post-production phase. Traditionally, editing has been one of the most time-consuming aspects of filmmaking. However, with AI-powered tools, editors can now automate routine tasks like sequencing scenes and stabilizing footage. This allows creatives to focus on the artistic side of editing, such as storytelling and emotional pacing. AI automates pattern recognition and sound synchronization, enabling even amateur editors to achieve professional results without extensive training. For example, Adobe Sensei uses machine learning to identify the best shots quickly, streamlining the editing process while maintaining high-quality standards. As a result, the democratization of editing through AI makes the art of filmmaking more accessible to a broader audience.

Visual effects (VFX) are another domain where AI is pushing creative boundaries by producing high-quality effects cost-effectively. In the past, creating realistic simulations required significant resources and time. Now, AI algorithms generate complex visual effects, from weather simulations to de-aging actors, at a fraction of the traditional costs. Disney's FaceDirector software, for example, was used in films like Avengers: Infinity War to perfect emotional expressions within CGI scenes, demonstrating how AI contributes to achieving realism otherwise unattainable.

Furthermore, audience analysis through AI provides filmmakers with powerful tools to predict audience reactions and refine marketing strategies. By examining social media data and viewing habits, AI can tailor films to specific demographics, making it possible to determine optimal release timings and platforms. This precision targeting is invaluable in maximizing viewership and return on investment. Platforms like Netflix use AI to curate personalized recommendations based on users' viewing history, enhancing engagement and satisfaction. This level of personalization ensures that films reach their intended audiences effectively, boosting both immediate and long-term success.

Incorporating AI into these crucial phases of filmmaking also addresses one of the industry's longstanding challenges: staying relevant and competitive. With AI tools providing actionable insights, studios can adapt to changing audience preferences swiftly, ensuring that they maintain a competitive edge. The integration of AI not only supports traditional methods but also introduces innovative approaches that broaden the creative possibilities available to filmmakers.

AI's role in the film industry doesn't stop at production; it's pivotal in distribution and audience engagement, transforming how films are marketed and consumed. By predicting box office outcomes and optimizing promotional efforts, AI helps studios maximize their resources and target potential viewers more accurately. In marketing campaigns, AI-driven analytics gauge audience sentiment, allowing marketers to adjust their strategies dynamically. An illustrative case is Warner Bros.'s use of AI in promoting Aquaman, which contributed significantly to its box office achievement.

7.3 Music and Art Generation Using AI

AI's emergence in the realm of music and art creation marks a transformative phase. It has begun to reshape traditional practices and opens up new avenues for creativity, offering tools that redefine what it means to be an artist or composer.

Let's start with AI composers, which have emerged as trailblazing entities capable of generating original tracks across diverse genres. This innovation empowers musicians by providing them a platform to experiment with sounds and styles that may have been beyond their reach in the past. By democratizing music creation, AI enables even those without formal musical training to craft unique compositions from the comfort of their homes. Through sophisticated algorithms, AI can analyze vast libraries of existing music, learning patterns and structures. An example is the Beatles-inspired song "Daddy's Car," where AI examined a selection of Beatles tracks and replicated their essence. While the song doesn't perfectly match the human touch of the originals, this demonstrates AI's potential to replicate and innovate within artistic confines, serving as both a collaborator and a competitor to traditional songwriting processes.

Transitioning to the visual arts, AI's role in art creation poses intriguing questions about authorship and originality. Traditional notions of what constitutes an artist are being challenged as AI systems like Google's DeepDream or the DALL-E 2 model produce stunning and complex artworks by interpreting text prompts or transforming existing images. These computational tools expand the range of artistic styles, suggesting new possibilities and redefining creative boundaries. Artists now find themselves collaborating with technology to achieve results that are dynamic and multifaceted, pushing the limits of conventional methods. This amalgamation of technology and artistry allows for exploration into realms previously deemed impossible—a fusion of human intuition and machine efficiency. For artists, AI serves not only as a tool but also as an inspiration, prompting further evolution of styles and concepts.

Enhanced music recommendations mark another significant development, powered by AI. Streaming services such as Spotify and Apple Music harness AI-driven algorithms to curate personalized listening experiences. By analyzing user listening habits, these platforms deliver suggestions tailored to individual preferences, strengthening the connection between artists and audiences. For musicians, this increases the discoverability of their work, allowing new songs to reach wider audiences than ever before. However, this wave of AI-generated content brings challenges; as Antonuccio explains, the sheer volume of music entering the marketplace can make standing out difficult for emerging artists. To navigate this landscape, creators must employ strategies that highlight their unique voices amidst the digital noise.

Finally, interactive art installations represent one of the most engaging applications of AI in art. These installations invite viewers to actively participate in the artistic process, creating dynamic pieces that respond to audience interaction. Such works often employ sensors and machine learning to adapt their behavior based on viewer movements or feedback, offering a different experience each time they are encountered. By being reactive and mutable, these interactive creations invoke deeper connections with their audiences, encouraging multiple interpretations and interactions. They epitomize how modern art can transcend static representation, becoming a living dialogue between creator, medium, and observer.

7.4 AI's Impact on Storytelling and Narrative Structures

Artificial intelligence (AI) is transforming the landscape of narrative design across various entertainment media, offering more interactive and immersive experiences than ever before. Central to this transformation is the development of adaptive narratives that tailor themselves to individual choices, thereby enhancing both engagement and personalization for audiences.

Adaptive narratives allow stories to evolve based on user decisions, leading to a personalized experience that is unique to each individual. This capability elevates storytelling from a passive activity to an interactive experience where the audience becomes an active participant in shaping the outcome. For instance, in video games or interactive films, players might choose a character's response in a crucial dialog or decide which path to take, with these choices directly influencing the story's progression. Such adaptability ensures that users remain engaged, as they're not merely spectators but integral parts of the unfolding narrative.

Character development significantly benefits from AI-generated dialogue, which adds depth by introducing varied conversational pathways influenced by user interaction. Traditional linear storytelling often struggles to present characters with realistic, evolving personalities. However, with AI, characters can respond dynamically, adapting their dialogue based on past interactions and future scenarios. This dynamism allows characters to display emotional complexity, making them more relatable and lifelike for users. In interactive fiction, for example, AI-driven dialogue can make characters react to player actions, further deepening immersion and connection between user and storyline.

Additionally, plot prediction algorithms are becoming invaluable tools for creators by analyzing successful narrative components. These algorithms sift through vast amounts of data from past stories, discerning patterns and elements that resonate most effectively with audiences. By identifying such trends, they enable creators to refine their storytelling techniques, thus improving efficiency and raising audience satisfaction levels. Filmmakers and writers can use these insights to tweak their narratives for better pacing and tension, ensuring they hit the right emotional beats at the correct moments.

Real-time narrative adjustments are another significant advancement brought about by AI. Through these capabilities, storytellers can incorporate immediate feedback into their content, allowing stories to swiftly resonate with contemporary audiences. This feature is especially valuable in digital and live-streamed content, where real-time user reactions can influence the direction a story takes. For example, during live gaming streams or interactive shows, audience responses may determine character arcs or plot outcomes, resulting in a deeply personalized experience that aligns closely with audience preferences.

Furthermore, the incorporation of artificial intelligence in narrative design promotes a new level of flexibility, granting creators the ability to experiment with unconventional story structures. By breaking away from traditional linear narratives, AI encourages branching storylines, multiple endings, and nonlinear plots, all tailored to audience engagement. This experimental freedom fosters creative innovation, enabling artists and developers to craft unique stories that push the boundaries of conventional media.

Moreover, AI-enhanced storytelling tools contribute to reduced production time and costs. Automated processes in creating dialogue, plotting, and even visual effects allow creators to allocate resources toward enhancing the quality of their work rather than getting bogged down in repetitive tasks. The efficiency gained through AI means storytellers can iterate on ideas quickly, refining their narratives with greater speed and precision.

From a business perspective, entertainment companies leveraging AI can deliver more engaging and efficient narrative experiences. By integrating AI-powered analytics, these companies gain insights into audience preferences and behaviors, allowing them to fine-tune content offerings effectively. This approach not only boosts user engagement but also leads to increased profitability by ensuring content aligns with market demands.

7.5 Ethical Considerations and Challenges of AI in Entertainment

In the evolving landscape of artificial intelligence, its integration into entertainment has sparked significant ethical and technical debates. One pressing concern is the threat of job displacement. As AI becomes more capable of performing tasks traditionally carried out by humans, there's a palpable fear within creative industries about workforce reduction. Automation in fields like animation, music production, and even storytelling could potentially replace human roles, leading to significant shifts in employment. This challenge underscores the need for workforce adaptation strategies. Reskilling programs are essential to help displaced workers transition into new roles that may arise as AI continues to transform these industries. By investing in education and training programs, industries can better equip their workforce to navigate technological advancements and mitigate potential unemployment.

Another pivotal topic is the question of content authenticity. With AI being increasingly used to generate art, music, and stories, the lines between human and machine creativity blur. Who holds the rights to an AI-generated piece? The ownership of such content becomes complex when a human feeds input into an AI system designed by someone else, producing a unique output. Moreover, this raises issues surrounding originality and intellectual property. Without clear guidelines, disputes over rights and commercial use can become common, complicating the process for creators and consumers alike.

Bias in AI algorithms is another crucial ethical issue. These algorithms often learn from existing datasets that may reflect societal biases, inadvertently perpetuating stereotypes. For instance, AI trained on historical data that lacks diversity might create biased outcomes, whether in selecting music, casting actors, or developing narratives. To tackle this, inclusive dataset practices must be implemented to ensure fair representation across all AI applications. This includes curating diverse and representative data sources, along with regular audits and updates to the algorithm's learning parameters, to actively counteract and reduce biases.

The evolution of regulatory frameworks is critical in addressing AI ethics. As AI technology rapidly advances, existing regulations struggle to keep pace. New guidelines are necessary to balance the benefits of innovation with responsible technology use. Regulatory bodies must work in tandem with AI developers to establish standards that safeguard against misuse while promoting ethical AI deployments. These frameworks should encompass data privacy, transparency in how AI systems operate, and accountability for AI-driven decisions. Establishing such regulations requires collaboration among technologists, policymakers, and ethicists to develop comprehensive strategies that uphold ethical principles in the deployment and usage of AI.

Finally, there's a broader societal impact of AI to consider. Beyond individual industries, AI's influence extends to shaping cultural norms and public opinion. Technologies like deepfakes, which can manipulate audiovisual content, present risks in terms of misinformation and social manipulation. The potential for AI-driven content to sway public perception underscores the imperative for vigilance and robust countermeasures. Ethical AI development must therefore include mechanisms for limiting the spread of false information and ensuring that AI systems contribute positively to society. By fostering transparency and encouraging open dialogue among stakeholders, we can better direct AI's capabilities towards beneficial outcomes.

7.6 Final Insights

In this chapter, we've journeyed through the fascinating world of AI's role in content creation and distribution. From procedural generation in gaming to script development in movies, AI is redefining creative processes. We've explored how intelligent NPCs in video games enhance engagement and how automation in film editing streamlines production. The impact of AI on these industries also extends to the art world, where it enables new forms of artistic expression and challenges traditional notions of creativity. Through adaptive narratives and personalized recommendations, AI not only transforms storytelling but also reshapes audience interaction, making experiences uniquely tailored and engaging.

As we look toward the future, the potential for AI to further revolutionize content creation across various media is immense. It stands as a tool that democratizes access to creativity, offering new possibilities for both seasoned professionals and newcomers. Embracing AI requires consideration of ethical implications, such as data privacy and authenticity, ensuring these advancements benefit society as a whole. By understanding AI's capabilities and implications, we equip ourselves to navigate this evolving landscape, ready to harness its power to craft more compelling stories, create dynamic virtual worlds, and deliver personalized experiences that resonate with diverse audiences.

Chapter 8: The Future of Work: Adapting to AI-Powered Jobs

Adapting to AI-powered jobs is an essential task in today's rapidly changing job market. AI technology has permeated various industries, redefining how work is done and the skills required for success. Navigating this shift can be daunting, but it also offers exciting opportunities for growth and innovation. By understanding the dynamics of AI integration, individuals and organizations can position themselves advantageously in this evolving landscape. This chapter delves into how artificial intelligence is reshaping workplaces, offering insights into what these changes mean for professionals across various fields.

In this chapter, we explore the new skill sets that are becoming indispensable in an AI-driven world. As roles evolve, critical thinking, data literacy, adaptability, and emotional intelligence emerge as key competencies. Discover how these skills empower individuals to harness AI's potential while maintaining a human touch in professional settings. The chapter further examines the creation of novel job roles thanks to AI advancements, shedding light on career paths that blend technical expertise with innovative thinking. Additionally, gain perspective on how educational institutions and employers can play pivotal roles in equipping future workers to excel in AI-enhanced environments. Through this exploration, you will gain a robust understanding of how to thrive in a workplace transformed by artificial intelligence, making the most of both your personal abilities and technological tools at your disposal.

8.1 Skills Needed in an AI-Driven World

As the job landscape becomes more intertwined with artificial intelligence, a shift in essential skills is necessary to thrive in this evolving environment. One of these foundational skills is critical thinking. This involves the ability to analyze and evaluate information, helping individuals solve complex problems effectively. In an AI-enhanced workplace, employees are often inundated with data generated by intelligent systems. Here, critical thinking enables them to sift through vast amounts of information, distinguish between relevant and irrelevant data, and make informed decisions that propel innovation and efficiency. Employers value workers who possess this skill because it empowers them to navigate uncharted territories and tackle challenges head-on without relying solely on algorithms.

Equally crucial is data literacy, which refers to understanding and utilizing data for decision-making processes across various industries. As organizations increasingly rely on AI to drive operations, the ability to interpret and leverage data becomes indispensable. Data literacy extends beyond mere familiarity with numbers; it encompasses comprehending trends, recognizing patterns, and applying insights to business strategies. For instance, in fields such as finance or healthcare, being data literate allows professionals to harness predictive analytics for risk assessment or personalized medicine. By empowering individuals to make data-driven decisions, organizations gain a competitive edge in the marketplace and reinforce their capacity for growth and innovation.

Adaptability emerges as another key skill in the context of AI-influenced work environments. The rapid pace of technological advancements means that professionals must continuously learn and adjust to new tools and methodologies. Adaptable workers can seamlessly transition between traditional and emerging technologies, ensuring they remain valuable assets within their organizations. This flexibility not only enhances individual productivity but also contributes to the overall resilience of a team. When faced with shifting priorities or unexpected challenges, adaptable employees are better equipped to devise creative solutions and maintain momentum.

Emotional intelligence stands out as a vital skill that enriches collaboration and interpersonal relationships in workplaces where AI takes over routine tasks. While machines excel at logic and efficiency, they lack the nuanced understanding of human emotions and motivations. Emotional intelligence fills this gap by enabling individuals to connect meaningfully with colleagues, fostering teamwork and communication. It involves being aware of one's own emotions, regulating them effectively, and empathizing with others. In leadership roles, emotional intelligence can be particularly valuable, allowing leaders to inspire trust and guide their teams through periods of change. As AI remains focused on analytical tasks, the human element provided by emotional intelligence ensures a balanced and harmonious work environment.

In integrating these skills, educational institutions play a pivotal role in preparing future workers for an AI-powered job market. By cultivating spaces where students can develop critical thinking through activities like debates and problem-solving exercises, educators equip them with the tools needed to excel. Encouraging data literacy programs demystifies technology, making it accessible to those without technical backgrounds. Offering courses that emphasize adaptability fosters a mindset open to lifelong learning and continuous improvement. Similarly, incorporating emotional intelligence training into curricula helps shape well-rounded individuals capable of thriving in dynamic and diverse workplaces.

The collective emphasis on these skills transforms individuals into holistic thinkers who see beyond immediate tasks and contribute strategically to their organizations. By investing in professional development, employers nurture a workforce that is not only proficient in navigating AI-enhanced environments but also adept at leveraging emerging technologies for business success. Employees, in turn, experience enhanced job satisfaction and personal fulfillment as they engage in meaningful work that aligns with their values.

Having outlined these essential skills, it becomes evident that each plays a unique yet interconnected role in shaping the workforce of the future. Critical thinking empowers individuals to approach problems analytically, while data literacy grounds decisions in empirical evidence. Adaptability ensures seamless integration with new technologies and resilience in the face of change. Meanwhile, emotional intelligence reinforces the human connections that underpin collaborative success. Together, these skills form a robust foundation for workers looking to thrive amid AI-led transformations.

For businesses, cultivating a culture that values and nurtures these skills is vital to remaining competitive in an era marked by constant innovation. By encouraging employees to embrace critical thinking, champion data literacy, exhibit adaptability, and practice emotional intelligence, organizations can cultivate a dynamic workforce poised to seize opportunities presented by the AI revolution. Such strategic foresight not only bolsters organizational growth but also positions companies as leaders in driving positive change within their respective industries.

8.2 New Job Roles Created by AI

In today's rapidly evolving job market, the integration of AI technologies is not only reshaping existing roles but also creating entirely new opportunities. This presents a compelling narrative of adaptation and innovation, especially in the face of AI's expanding influence across various sectors.

One of the key roles emerging in this new landscape is that of an AI trainer. These professionals are crucial in teaching AI systems how to perform specific tasks effectively. AI trainers are responsible for continuously updating these systems to ensure proficiency and efficiency as demands evolve. They work closely with data scientists and machine learning experts, providing real-world data that can help fine-tune algorithms.

By bridging the gap between human intelligence and machine learning, AI trainers play a pivotal role in maintaining the relevance of AI applications in industries ranging from customer service to advanced computing.

Parallel to the technical advancements driven by AI trainers, AI ethicists emerge as guardians of moral integrity within the technological realm. Their role is to evaluate the ethical implications of AI deployment and offer guidance for its responsible integration into society. With AI's potential to perpetuate biases or infringe on privacy, the insights provided by AI ethicists aid in crafting policies and practices that prioritize equality and transparency. As highlighted by workplace trends, these roles will likely expand as more organizations recognize the necessity for ethical oversight in their AI strategies.

Data curators are another integral component in the constellation of new AI-driven career paths. Their work involves managing and refining the data inputs that AI models rely on, ensuring accuracy and reliability. Inaccurate or biased data can lead to faulty outcomes in AI applications, making the role of data curators essential for the success of any AI initiative. These specialists meticulously organize and audit datasets, working to eliminate inconsistencies and biases. Through their efforts, they elevate the precision of AI systems, reinforcing trust in AI solutions deployed across sectors like finance, healthcare, and beyond.

Moreover, as AI becomes more integrated into our daily lives, the role of human-AI interaction designers gains prominence. These designers are tasked with creating user-friendly interfaces that facilitate seamless human-AI collaboration. Their objective is to ensure that AI tools are accessible and intuitive, enabling users to interact with them effortlessly. By focusing on enhancing the usability of AI systems, human-AI interaction designers help amplify the productivity and satisfaction of end-users in diverse settings, including workplaces and smart homes. Their work often involves employing user-centric design principles to develop interfaces that bridge the gap between complex AI functionalities and everyday users.

As AI transforms various sectors, these emerging roles highlight the dynamic interplay between technology and human expertise. AI trainers, ethicists, data curators, and interaction designers are not just adapting to change—they are driving it, shaping the future of work in ways that align with ethical standards and practical needs. This convergence of skills underscores a broader trend where jobs of the future demand a fusion of technical prowess and human insight. For those venturing into this evolving landscape, embracing these roles presents an opportunity to be at the forefront of innovation.

8.3 AI in Remote Work and Virtual Collaborations

AI is transforming the way remote teams collaborate and execute tasks, revolutionizing how businesses function. The integration of AI-driven collaboration tools is enhancing real-time communication and project management for distributed teams, crucially supporting the shift towards remote work environments. These tools are designed to streamline workflows by automating routine processes and ensuring that team members remain connected, regardless of their geographical locations.

Collaboration tools powered by AI play a pivotal role by facilitating seamless communication among team members who may be scattered across different time zones or continents. By providing features like instant messaging, video conferencing, and file sharing on a unified platform, these tools allow teams to interact efficiently as though they were co-located in a physical office space. This connectivity minimizes the potential for miscommunication and keeps everyone on the same page regarding project objectives and timelines.

Performance monitoring systems driven by AI offer businesses the ability to track employee productivity remotely. These systems can analyze patterns in work output, identify areas for improvement, and deliver feedback based on objective data points. However, this capability raises significant privacy concerns, as employees may feel constantly observed or evaluated, leading to stress or decreased morale.

To balance monitoring with privacy, companies must establish transparent policies about data usage and involve employees in discussions about how these systems function. This approach fosters trust while leveraging the benefits of AI to enhance productivity without compromising personal privacy.

Virtual assistants are another crucial component of AI's impact on remote workflows. They manage administrative tasks such as scheduling meetings, setting reminders, and answering frequently asked questions (FAQ), freeing up team members to focus on more strategic activities. By handling routine queries and facilitating seamless coordination, virtual assistants reduce the cognitive burden on workers, enabling them to concentrate on high-priority projects.

Guidelines for effectively utilizing virtual assistants include training team members on how to interact with these tools, regularly updating their knowledge base, and ensuring they integrate smoothly with existing workflows. This maximizes the efficiency gains from automation while maintaining effective human oversight.

Personalized learning through AI is reshaping professional development for remote workers by tailoring training programs to individual needs. AI analyzes an employee's skills, preferences, and performance history to recommend targeted training modules, ensuring relevance and engagement. This personalized approach not only helps workers acquire new skills but also boosts motivation by addressing each individual's career aspirations.

Creating customized learning paths involves collaborating with training providers and leveraging AI analytics to continuously assess and adjust courses based on learner feedback and progress. Organizations benefit from a more skilled workforce, while employees gain opportunities for growth and advancement.

8.4 AI's Impact on Traditional Industries

AI is reshaping traditional industries by enhancing the way operations are conducted, leading to significant transformations across manufacturing, healthcare, and finance. In this exploration, we'll delve into how AI's integration is optimizing these sectors and discuss the evolving skill sets required to thrive in an AI-driven world.

In the manufacturing industry, AI improves efficiency by leveraging predictive maintenance and quality control. Predictive maintenance involves using AI algorithms to analyze data from IoT sensors embedded in machinery. This analysis helps identify potential equipment failures before they occur, minimizing downtime and reducing repair costs. For example, companies like General Electric use AI-powered systems that predict machine failures up to six months in advance, allowing them to schedule maintenance at the most convenient times. Additionally, AI enhances quality control through computer vision technology, which inspects products for defects with greater accuracy and speed than human inspectors can achieve. This ensures that only high-quality products reach customers, thereby increasing customer satisfaction and brand reputation.

Healthcare is another sector experiencing a profound transformation due to AI. AI assists in diagnostics by analyzing medical images and patient data to detect abnormalities and diseases more accurately and quickly than traditional methods. IBM Watson, for instance, uses AI to aid oncologists in identifying cancerous tumors by analyzing vast datasets of medical literature and imaging studies, improving diagnostic accuracy. Personalized medicine is another area where AI plays a critical role, as it enables physicians to tailor treatment plans based on individual genetic profiles and lifestyle factors. Moreover, AI applications in patient care management streamline hospital workflows, reduce administrative burdens, and improve patient outcomes by ensuring timely interventions and efficient resource allocation.

In the finance sector, AI is revolutionizing operations by enhancing fraud detection, algorithmic trading, and personalized customer service. AI algorithms can detect unusual transaction patterns indicative of fraudulent activity, enabling financial institutions to respond swiftly and prevent losses. JP Morgan Chase employs AI to analyze billions of transactions in real-time, significantly reducing fraud incidents and saving millions annually. Algorithmic trading, powered by AI, processes vast amounts of market data to execute trades with precision and speed, optimizing investment returns for firms and individual investors alike. Furthermore, AI-driven chatbots and virtual assistants offer personalized financial advice, catering to individual needs and preferences while enhancing customer experience.

As AI becomes integral to these traditional sectors, workers are prompted to adapt by acquiring new skills to remain competitive. The demand for tech-savvy professionals who understand AI tools and applications is growing rapidly. For example, in manufacturing, employees are trained to operate and maintain AI-driven machinery, while healthcare professionals must learn to interpret AI-generated insights for patient care. In finance, personnel need to comprehend AI algorithms and their implications for trading strategies and customer interactions. Consequently, individuals must embrace continuous learning and develop technical proficiency alongside soft skills like critical thinking and problem-solving.

To effectively navigate an AI-driven landscape, workers should focus on building a robust understanding of AI technologies and their applications within specific industries. Developing expertise in data analysis, machine learning, and programming languages can prove valuable, as these skills enable individuals to harness AI's potential and drive innovation in their respective fields. Additionally, staying informed about current trends and advancements in AI will allow professionals to anticipate changes and adapt accordingly.

8.5 Challenges and Ethical Considerations

In today's rapidly evolving job market, the integration of artificial intelligence (AI) into the workforce presents both exciting possibilities and significant challenges. As AI continues to reshape industries, a primary concern that emerges is the potential for job displacement. Automation of routine tasks by AI systems is creating anxiety among workers who fear their roles may become obsolete. While AI is undoubtedly efficient at handling repetitive tasks, it's crucial for businesses and policymakers to balance technological advancement with workforce stability. Retraining programs and continuous education initiatives can help workers transition into new roles that require human creativity and critical thinking—skills that machines cannot replicate.

Beyond job displacement, ethical considerations around AI use in the workplace are gaining prominence. Transparency in AI decision-making processes is essential for cultivating trust among employees and customers alike. Ethical AI demands that organizations clearly communicate how AI tools operate and make decisions, ensuring accountability and reducing fears about so-called "black box" algorithms. When individuals understand the basis of AI-driven conclusions or actions, it fosters a sense of control and partnership rather than apprehension.

Another pressing issue is the presence of biases within AI algorithms. Since these systems often learn from historical data, there's a risk they may perpetuate existing stereotypes or inequities. Addressing these biases requires rigorous scrutiny of training datasets and continuous updates to models to ensure fair and inclusive outcomes. For instance, hiring platforms utilizing AI must be vigilant against reinforcing gender or racial biases present in past recruitment data. By prioritizing fairness, organizations can leverage AI technologies to support diversity and inclusivity in the workforce.

Moreover, as AI becomes more embedded in daily operations, regulatory frameworks must evolve to address privacy and security concerns. AI's effectiveness often relies on vast amounts of personal data, raising questions about how this information is stored and used. Implementing robust data governance policies is vital to protect individual privacy rights while harnessing AI's capabilities. Additionally, regulations should ensure that AI applications do not compromise user security by introducing vulnerabilities or facilitating unauthorized data access.

8.6 Final Insights

As we wrap up this chapter, it's clear that AI is reshaping the job landscape in profound ways. We've delved into how critical skills like adaptability, data literacy, and emotional intelligence are becoming essential in an AI-driven world. These skills enable individuals to work effectively alongside AI, ensuring they remain valuable in their fields. By understanding how these roles evolve and how AI creates new opportunities, we can see the importance of continuous learning in staying ahead. AI isn't just changing what jobs exist; it's altering how we approach our careers and professional growth.

For businesses and professionals alike, embracing this change is key to thriving in the future. Companies need to foster a culture that values these emerging skills, supporting employees as they adapt to new roles created by AI. On a personal level, keeping informed about AI's developments and being open to acquiring new competencies will be crucial. Whether you're just starting in the workforce or are a seasoned professional, navigating these changes with curiosity and flexibility can lead to exciting possibilities. Overall, the synergy between human capability and AI technology stands to redefine not just individual careers but entire industries, heralding a new era of innovation and collaboration.

Chapter 9: Beginner-Friendly AI Tools: Getting Hands-On

Getting hands-on with beginner-friendly AI tools opens up endless possibilities for anyone interested in this exciting field. These tools are designed to make artificial intelligence accessible, allowing users from various backgrounds to explore and engage with AI technologies without feeling overwhelmed. As the demand for AI skills grows across industries, having a solid foundation can be invaluable. Whether you're just curious about what AI can offer, or you're looking to integrate it into your work or studies, understanding how to start using these tools is key. They demystify the complex nature of AI by offering user-friendly interfaces, tutorials, and projects tailored specifically for beginners, ensuring that learning about AI is engaging rather than intimidating.

The chapter delves into some of the most accessible AI tools available today, ideal for those new to the technology. It highlights platforms like CodeEasy AI and No-Code AI Playground, demonstrating how they simplify the AI learning curve through intuitive design and practical examples. You'll also learn about task-specific applications such as SmartFlow Manager and

TimeSync AI that enhance productivity by automating daily tasks. The chapter further explores collaborative tools like CollabAI Hub, which emphasizes the importance of teamwork in AI projects. By examining these tools and their potential applications, this chapter aims to equip you with the knowledge to confidently take your first steps in the AI landscape, empowering you to leverage artificial intelligence effectively in personal and professional contexts.

9.1 Introduction to AI Coding Platforms

Exploring the world of artificial intelligence (AI) can seem a bit daunting, especially for those new to coding. Yet, with the right tools, beginners can start their AI journey with ease and confidence. Coding platforms designed specifically for novice users make it possible to dip your toes into AI without being overwhelmed by technical jargon or complex programming languages.

One standout platform is CodeEasy AI, which offers a beginner-friendly environment tailored for those with minimal coding experience. What makes CodeEasy so approachable is its focus on simplicity. Rather than throwing users into the depths of advanced coding, it covers only the basics necessary to get started with AI projects. Imagine a place where you can create simple models or run basic scripts without having to learn an entirely new language from scratch. This approach not only minimizes frustration but also builds foundational skills that can be expanded later as confidence grows.

While CodeEasy eases users into coding, No-Code AI Playground takes a slightly different approach by offering an entirely visual programming experience. Visual programming allows learners to understand AI concepts through intuitive graphical interfaces instead of traditional code. Users can drag and drop elements to create AI models, providing immediate feedback and making it easier to grasp complex ideas. For example, you might use blocks representing data inputs, processing steps, and outputs to construct your AI workflow visually. This method demystifies how AI models function, sparking curiosity and reducing the intimidation factor often associated with coding.

Moving beyond introductory platforms, the AI Starter Suite shines by offering templates and compatibility with various libraries. This feature-rich platform caters to a diverse range of interests and levels of expertise. Beginners can utilize pre-made templates for common AI tasks like image recognition or natural language processing, allowing them to quickly see results without extensive setup. Furthermore, as users grow more adept, they can explore the suite's library compatibility to customize their projects. Imagine starting with a template model, then gradually modifying it by integrating additional libraries to expand its capabilities. This adaptability ensures continuous learning and keeps the door open for more complex projects in the future.

In addition to individual exploration, collaboration is crucial in the AI field. CollabAI Hub emerges as a valuable tool, facilitating teamwork and leveraging cloud resources to enhance the learning experience. Collaboration can transform solitary study into a community effort, where sharing knowledge and resources accelerates progress. With CollabAI Hub, users can seamlessly work together on projects, contribute unique insights, and collectively troubleshoot challenges. The integration of cloud resources means that even computationally demanding tasks can be managed efficiently, without the need for expensive hardware. Picture a scenario where you're collaborating on an AI project with fellow learners around the globe, each contributing their strengths to achieve a common goal. This synergy not only enriches the learning process but mirrors real-world AI development environments.

By now, you may be wondering how these platforms fit into broader goals and applications. They serve as gateways, not just to understanding AI theoretically, but to harnessing its potential for personal and professional growth. Whether you aim to boost productivity, drive innovation in business, or pursue a career in technology, starting with these beginner-friendly tools can set you on the right path.

The beauty of these platforms is their ability to accommodate various learning styles and paces. Some learners thrive on structured guidance, while others prefer experiential hands-on exploration. These tools ensure that regardless of your preference, there's room to experiment and grow. Envision yourself navigating through different platforms, choosing the one that resonates most with your learning style, and gradually building competence through trial and error.

As you venture into these tools, remember that the journey into AI isn't a sprint; it's a marathon. Each step taken on platforms like CodeEasy AI, No-Code AI Playground, AI Starter Suite, and

CollabAI Hub builds a stronger foundation for understanding AI's intricacies. Over time, what seemed complex and unattainable becomes a set of manageable challenges, leading to deeper engagement with the material.

Moreover, the collaborative nature of many of these platforms means that you're never truly alone in your learning process. You'll find forums, user communities, and expert guidance readily available, all eager to share insights and support your journey. Such connections are invaluable, providing real-world context and making AI less about theory and more about practical application.

9.2 AI Apps and Tools for Personal Productivity

Exploring AI applications that can enhance personal productivity is an exciting journey, especially for those new to this technological advancement. Imagine having a digital assistant that learns your habits and needs, helping you manage time effectively, stay organized, and boost creativity. Let's dive into how some AI tools can make this happen with ease.

First up is SmartFlow Manager, a tool that revolutionizes how we handle daily tasks. This AI employs intelligent algorithms to prioritize tasks based on user input, ensuring that your day runs smoothly without you feeling overwhelmed. Imagine waking up each morning to a perfectly organized schedule that adapts to your priorities. SmartFlow Manager takes note of your most important tasks and structures your day accordingly. Whether you have deadlines approaching or meetings scheduled, this tool adjusts dynamically, providing reminders and rearranging tasks as needed. It even suggests optimal times to tackle certain tasks, boosting efficiency and preventing burnout. For beginners, using such tools can be a game-changer in managing work-life balance effectively.

Similarly, TimeSync AI transforms the way you manage your schedule by analyzing your daily habits and recommending the best times for various activities. Consider this your personal scheduling expert that knows when you're most productive, allowing it to suggest optimal working hours and breaks. TimeSync AI collects data on your behavior throughout the day, including when you tend to be most active, and uses this information to craft a schedule tailored just for you. Over time, it identifies patterns—like when you're typically free or busy—and provides suggestions on how to use your time more efficiently. This feature is particularly invaluable for business professionals who juggle numerous commitments and need precise time management to meet all their goals.

Next, BudgetWise AI simplifies the often daunting task of managing finances. By automating budgeting activities and offering personalized financial insights, this tool becomes an indispensable companion for anyone looking to improve their money management skills without needing an accountancy degree. BudgetWise AI tracks spending, categorizes expenses, and highlights areas where you might be overspending. With its help, setting and maintaining budgets becomes straight-forward. Furthermore, BudgetWise AI provides insightful reports and alerts that allow you to make informed financial decisions. This kind of support enables you to effortlessly align your spending with your long-term financial goals, making budgeting less of a chore and more of an empowering activity.

WriteGenius AI, on the other hand, opens up new possibilities for content creation. This AI-powered assistant enhances writing endeavors by automating editing processes and adapting style preferences. Whether you're drafting a business report or crafting a blog post, WriteGenius AI ensures that your content stands out with clarity and style. The tool reviews text for grammar and syntax errors, offers rephrasing suggestions, and aligns content with your specified tone and voice. For students or tech enthusiasts, WriteGenius AI serves as a valuable resource that helps develop writing skills by providing immediate feedback and style recommendations.

These AI tools demonstrate how technology can seamlessly integrate into daily routines, enhancing productivity without overwhelming users with complicated systems. For beginners, these tools offer a gateway into the world of AI without needing prior technical expertise. They present an opportunity to experience firsthand how AI can transform routine activities and provide tangible benefits in everyday life.

Moreover, entrepreneurs and freelancers find particular value in these tools as they optimize workflows and maximize efficiency. For instance, an entrepreneur using SmartFlow Manager and TimeSync AI could streamline operations and focus on strategic growth, while BudgetWise AI aids in making smarter financial choices. Freelancers can leverage WriteGenius AI to refine proposals and deliver polished content consistently, giving them a competitive edge in their respective fields.

9.3 Resources for Starting AI Projects

Diving into artificial intelligence (AI) can be daunting for beginners, but with the right tools and resources, anyone can embark on this exciting journey. To start AI projects confidently, several beginner-friendly resources are available to guide you through building foundational knowledge, fostering community interaction, and exploring creative applications.

One invaluable resource is the AI Bootcamp Online, which provides structured courses designed to lay a strong foundation in AI. These bootcamps often offer step-by-step instructions and hands-on projects that help learners grasp the basics of machine learning and data analysis. Participants engage with practical exercises using Python, one of the most popular programming languages in AI today. Courses typically cover essential topics such as data manipulation with pandas, a powerful open-source data analysis tool, and how to utilize Jupyter Notebook for recording and sharing analysis. With guided projects, beginners learn not only to write and execute code but also to interpret results critically and effectively apply their learning to real-world problems. This structured approach ensures that newcomers gain both theoretical understanding and practical experience, significantly boosting confidence as they progress in their AI journey.

Another crucial element for beginners is engagement within a supportive community, which is where the AI Connect Forum comes into play. This platform fosters discussion and collaboration among individuals who share an interest in AI, providing a space for dialogue about the latest trends, breakthroughs, and challenges in the field. Through forums and community-led projects, newcomers can pose questions, share insights, or even collaborate on AI initiatives. The interactive nature of these forums allows for diverse perspectives and solutions, enriching users' understanding and encouraging innovative thinking. Participating in community discussions also helps build a network of like-minded individuals who can offer support and guidance throughout one's learning journey, enhancing both personal growth and collective knowledge within the AI domain.

For those interested in furthering their understanding through reading, The AI Bookshelf serves as an excellent resource. This curated selection includes both theoretical and practical materials, catering to a variety of learning preferences and needs. The Bookshelf features foundational texts on machine learning algorithms, neural networks, and natural language processing, offering readers a comprehensive view of how machines interpret human language and solve complex problems. By delving into these materials, learners develop critical thinking skills and gain a deeper understanding of AI principles, enabling them to draw connections between theory and practice. In addition to classic textbooks, The AI Bookshelf might include case studies and biographies of AI pioneers, providing inspiration and context for the technology's evolution and potential future developments.

Experimentation and creativity are vital components of learning AI, and the OpenAI Toolbox is an ideal resource for hands-on exploration. It introduces users to a suite of open-source tools that encourage experimentation with AI models and frameworks, allowing for creative adaptations and personalized solutions. Users can experiment with TensorFlow and PyTorch, two leading frameworks in AI research and development, to create custom models tailored to specific tasks or projects. This toolbox empowers learners to push boundaries and innovate, exploring new applications for AI technologies. Moreover, engaging with open-source communities provides opportunities for feedback and improvement, as well as exposure to cutting-edge ideas and practices. Experimenting with these tools facilitates experiential learning, helping individuals connect theoretical insights with practical implementations, thereby strengthening their problem-solving capabilities and technical proficiency.

9.4 Exploring Community Support in AI Learning

In the journey to understand and implement artificial intelligence (AI), the role of community support cannot be overstated. As an individual delves into AI, especially beginners and those without a technical background, being part of a supportive ecosystem becomes invaluable. It acts as a bridge, linking enthusiasts with experts, facilitating learning, and fostering innovation in AI projects.

Community forums like AI Connect serve as vibrant hubs where people with diverse skill levels come together to share their knowledge and experiences. Such platforms allow users to interact with peers, which is crucial for knowledge exchange and collaboration on AI projects. For instance, a budding developer might face challenges while working on a machine-learning model. By engaging on these forums, they can gain insights from experienced users who have tackled similar issues, thus accelerating their learning process. The collaborative aspect of these communities not only enhances individual growth but also contributes to the collective advancement of AI technologies.

Additionally, community-driven platforms offer a unique environment where feedback is both plentiful and constructive. When individuals post their projects or ideas, they receive input from various community members who provide different perspectives. This constant flow of feedback encourages continual improvement, urging developers to refine their models and algorithms. John Doe, a novice entering the AI space, might initially struggle with creating efficient neural networks. However, by sharing his journey and receiving targeted advice from seasoned practitioners within these communities, he continuously hones his skills, ultimately leading to the creation of more optimized and effective AI solutions.

Regular webinars and discussions organized by AI communities are another cornerstone of learning. These events provide real-time updates on current AI innovations and methodologies, ensuring participants stay abreast of the latest trends and developments in the field. They offer a platform where industry leaders and researchers present cutting-edge advancements, thereby enabling learners to explore new concepts and applications. For example, a webinar discussing the integration of AI in healthcare can spark interest among professionals looking to apply intelligent systems in medical diagnostics, inspiring them to undertake projects within this domain.

Moreover, community resources complement structured learning programs by offering real-world insights and applications. While formal education lays down the foundational knowledge, interacting with community resources such as tutorials, shared repositories, and open-source toolkits provides practical experience that is crucial in mastering AI technologies. Students engaged in these communities often find themselves working on projects that simulate real-world scenarios, which aids in grasping complex theories by seeing their practical significance.

QuadC highlights the transformative power of online learning communities by emphasizing how these platforms enhance collaboration and support among learners. For instance, the student success features provided by QuadC enable not just the acquisition of knowledge but also the application of learned concepts in meaningful ways, demonstrating the critical role of community support in educational success. Learners gain access to diverse viewpoints and methodologies, broadening their understanding and pushing the boundaries of traditional education.

9.5 Practical Applications of Beginner-Friendly AI Tools

Exploring the world of artificial intelligence (AI) can initially seem overwhelming, especially for those without a technical background. However, as AI technology continues to advance and permeate various aspects of our lives, user-friendly tools have emerged to make this revolutionary field accessible to everyone. These tools help both individuals and businesses gain hands-on experience with AI projects, allowing them to see tangible results with minimal fuss.

One such platform is CodeEasy AI, designed specifically with beginners in mind. It provides users with an opportunity to learn through doing, which is invaluable for grasping AI concepts. By creating a space where users can experiment without fear of making mistakes, CodeEasy AI transforms the daunting task of understanding AI into an engaging, educational experience. Similarly, No-Code AI Playground enables users to build projects without needing extensive programming knowledge. By utilizing visual programming techniques, this platform breaks down complex AI processes into manageable steps, making AI concepts more digestible. This user-friendly approach ensures that anyone, regardless of their technical prowess, can participate in AI development.

Moreover, pre-built models and templates available on these platforms significantly speed up the development process. These resources remove many barriers traditionally associated with AI projects. Beginners can now focus on applying these models to real-world problems rather than getting bogged down in intricate coding challenges. This not only reduces the learning curve but also empowers users to implement AI solutions efficiently. The availability of these customizable templates means that even those new to AI can achieve meaningful outcomes quickly, boosting their confidence and encouraging further exploration.

Task-specific tools like BudgetWise AI exemplify how AI can enhance personal and professional efficiency. This tool automates budgeting tasks, providing personalized financial analyses that help users manage their finances more effectively. With BudgetWise AI, financial planning becomes a streamlined process, allowing users to allocate their time and resources more effectively. Such tools highlight AI's capability to handle repetitive tasks, enabling people to concentrate on areas where human insight is irreplaceable. This not only optimizes workflow but also illustrates AI's potential to support everyday activities, thus reinforcing its practical value.

The impact of beginner-friendly AI tools becomes even more evident when we consider real-life examples of successful AI projects. These success stories serve as powerful motivators, inspiring users to pursue their AI interests with renewed vigor. Whether it's a student developing a project that solves community issues or a small business using AI to enhance customer service, these examples underscore the transformative power of AI tools. They show how creativity, paired with accessible technology, can lead to innovative solutions that benefit both individuals and society at large.

In addition, these stories provide relatable narratives, demonstrating that successful AI applications aren't reserved for tech giants alone. Instead, they affirm that with the right tools and a bit of ingenuity, anyone can leverage AI to address challenges that matter to them. Such examples empower users by illustrating what is possible and encouraging them to explore AI's potential fully.

As you embark on your AI journey, remember that these beginner-friendly tools are crafted to demystify AI and bring it within reach. They foster an environment where experimentation and innovation thrive, turning complex concepts into achievable projects. By embracing these resources, users from various backgrounds can contribute to and reap the benefits of AI advancements. Whether you're looking to optimize business operations, tackle personal challenges, or ignite educational projects, these tools open doors to endless possibilities.

Ultimately, as AI continues to evolve, its accessibility remains a crucial factor in driving widespread adoption. Platforms like CodeEasy AI and No-Code AI Playground play a vital role in this mission by breaking down technical barriers and empowering users with practical skills. Pre-built models streamline initial efforts, while task-specific tools like BudgetWise AI showcase AI's ability to enhance day-to-day tasks. Real-world success stories then complete this narrative, demonstrating AI's tangible, positive impact.

9.6 Final Insights

As you wrap up this exploration of accessible AI tools for personal use, it's clear that these platforms offer a gateway to understanding and utilizing AI in a practical, approachable way. Throughout the chapter, we've delved into how tools like CodeEasy AI and No-Code AI Playground provide a gentle introduction to AI concepts by allowing users to create and experiment without needing extensive technical knowledge. These resources help demystify AI, showing learners that embarking on their AI journey doesn't have to be intimidating. With user-friendly interfaces and pre-built templates, beginners are empowered to dive into projects confidently, harnessing AI's potential to solve problems and enhance personal productivity.

Connecting these insights to real-world applications, the chapter highlighted how specific tools like SmartFlow Manager and BudgetWise AI can transform everyday tasks. Whether it's optimizing your schedule or simplifying financial management, these applications illustrate AI's ability to integrate seamlessly into daily life. Moreover, the collaborative nature of platforms such as CollabAI Hub emphasizes the importance of community support, encouraging shared learning and innovation. By leveraging these beginner-friendly tools, readers are invited to not only learn but also actively participate in AI's evolving landscape. Whether you're a student, professional, entrepreneur, or simply curious about AI, these insights illuminate a path where technology becomes both accessible and impactful, leading to numerous opportunities for growth and innovation.

Chapter 10: Ethical Considerations in AI: Navigating Challenges

Navigating the ethical landscape of artificial intelligence (AI) is a journey filled with challenges and complexities. As AI continues to merge into everyday life, it brings forth significant ethical dilemmas that require thoughtful consideration and valuable insight. These dilemmas often pivot around the fairness and impartiality of AI systems. Recognizing bias and ensuring equitable outcomes are crucial in preventing technology from reinforcing existing societal inequalities. This chapter sets out to explore these critical topics, illustrating how biases embedded in AI can influence sectors ranging from employment to criminal justice.

In this exploration, you will gain insights into various strategies to mitigate bias and promote fairness within AI systems. The chapter delves into the importance of using diverse data sets to train AI models, aiming for more balanced and representative outcomes. It highlights the role of standard metrics in evaluating fairness, offering frameworks to measure disparities and ensure ethical decision-making. Furthermore, the discussion extends to the potential business impacts of biased AI, emphasizing the legal and reputational risks companies face if they overlook these concerns. By the end of this chapter, you'll have a comprehensive understanding of the ethical considerations essential in developing responsible AI technologies, alongside practical approaches to addressing these pressing issues.

10.1 Bias and Fairness in AI Systems

Bias in AI systems can perpetuate unfair outcomes, and this problem is particularly concerning when it affects marginalized communities. Bias occurs when the data used to train AI models reflects existing prejudices, leading these systems to make decisions that reinforce those biases. A notable example is AI recruitment tools favoring resumes that resemble past successful candidates, typically male, due to gender imbalances in tech industry data. Similarly, in criminal justice, algorithms like COMPAS have shown racial bias by inaccurately assessing risk levels for defendants based on race.

Recognizing these disparities highlights the importance of implementing strategies to mitigate bias. One effective solution is the use of diverse data sets. By incorporating a wide range of demographic groups and scenarios into training data, AI systems can become more balanced and equitable. This approach ensures that AI does not inadvertently prioritize or discriminate against certain groups while also reflecting societal changes over time. Regularly updating data sets helps avoid outdated biases and supports the development of fairer AI outcomes.

In addition to diverse data collection, establishing standard metrics to evaluate fairness in AI is crucial. These metrics provide a framework to assess whether AI decision-making processes meet ethical standards. Fairness metrics allow developers and stakeholders to measure disparities in outcomes and guide necessary adjustments. For instance, adversarial testing can uncover biases by simulating edge cases that may not be apparent in standard testing. Through these evaluations, AI systems become more transparent and accountable.

High-profile controversies surrounding AI ethics underscore the significance of addressing bias. These incidents often surface in industries where AI technology has profound impacts, such as employment, finance, and law enforcement. When biases are exposed in these contexts, they can erode public trust in AI systems and hinder their adoption. Companies risk legal penalties and reputational damage if they fail to address these challenges responsibly.

To ensure AI technologies promote fairness, businesses and developers have a social responsibility to act ethically. They should strive to create AI systems that benefit society, rather than reinforcing existing inequalities. This involves being proactive in identifying potential sources of bias and taking steps to mitigate them from the outset. Implementing algorithmic fairness techniques, such as re-weighting data to better represent underrepresented groups, can help create more balanced AI models. These techniques aim to produce models that make equitable decisions across different demographic groups.

Moreover, transparency and accountability are essential in the

AI decision-making process. Making AI operations clear and understandable empowers users to trust these technologies. Transparent practices include disclosing how AI systems reach decisions and what factors influence those decisions. Engaging with diverse stakeholders, including ethicists and community leaders, can enhance understanding of bias issues and drive the creation of ethical AI frameworks.

The business impact of biased AI cannot be understated. Poor decisions driven by AI bias can lead to negative consequences for companies, such as decreased customer satisfaction and flawed strategic planning. For example, an AI system trained on biased data might deny loans to applicants from specific zip codes without considering individual circumstances, resulting in unjust outcomes. Addressing AI bias not only prevents such errors but also contributes to building trust with consumers and clients.

Legal responsibilities further raise the stakes for managing AI bias. Companies using biased AI systems could face regulatory scrutiny and potential lawsuits. It becomes imperative for businesses to align AI technologies with existing laws and ethical standards to avoid these pitfalls. As AI continues to evolve and integrate across various sectors, staying informed about legal obligations is crucial for sustaining ethical AI practices.

10.2 Privacy Concerns with AI Data

In today's digital age, AI has become an integral part of how personal data is handled, raising significant privacy concerns. As AI technologies permeate various aspects of our lives, understanding how they interact with personal data is crucial for ensuring user trust and compliance with privacy regulations. This exploration begins with the transparency— or lack thereof—in data collection practices.

A major concern in AI's engagement with personal data is the opacity surrounding data collection. Often, users are unaware of how much of their personal information is being collected, stored, and utilized by AI systems. This lack of transparency can lead to a fundamental mistrust between users and organizations that employ AI, as consumers feel left in the dark regarding the extent of surveillance they are under. Trust issues arise when individuals realize that their data might be aggregated not just for service improvement but also for less ethical uses such as targeted advertising or even selling data to third parties. The fear of misuse or unfair treatment based on collected data fosters suspicion, further widened by incidents where inadequately secured data is leaked or hacked.

The vulnerabilities of AI systems to cyberattacks also accentuate these privacy concerns. AI, with its vast pools of personal data, presents an attractive target for cybercriminals. Without robust security measures, sensitive data such as financial details, personal identifiers, and private communications are at risk of exposure. Cybersecurity breaches not only compromise individuals' privacy but can also have ramifications on a wider scale, affecting entire networks and systems. Organizations must, therefore, prioritize implementing stringent security protocols to protect data against unauthorized access and breaches. Regular updates and process evaluations should be a norm to ensure ongoing resilience against evolving cyber threats.

To navigate these challenges effectively, it is imperative to understand regulatory frameworks like the General Data Protection Regulation (GDPR) and the California Consumer Privacy Act (CCPA). These laws aim to safeguard individuals' privacy rights, offering a legal backbone to protect data from unauthorized use and exploitation. GDPR, for instance, grants EU citizens the right to access their data, request corrections, and demand deletion if necessary. Similarly, CCPA empowers California residents to know what personal data is being collected about them and to opt-out of the sale of their information. Such regulations underscore the importance of data privacy and inform users of their rights, thereby fostering a landscape where transparency is prioritized.

Beyond relying on regulations, there is also the pivotal role of user activism in shaping data ethics. Awareness and utilization of privacy tools empower individuals to take control over their data. Tools like browser extensions for blocking trackers, encrypted communication apps, and password managers are becoming increasingly recognized as essential for safeguarding privacy. The collective efforts of informed users advocating for better privacy standards can drive significant social change. When businesses perceive a strong demand for ethical data practices, propelled by educated and vocal consumers, they are more likely to adapt accordingly.

Mitigation strategies are necessary to address concerns around AI and data privacy. Organizations should strive for transparency, making their data collection policies clear and accessible. Implementing data minimization techniques—only collecting data that is absolutely necessary—is another essential step towards protecting privacy. Moreover, introducing differential privacy, which allows datasets to be analyzed without revealing individual information, could significantly enhance user trust.

10.3 Accountability in AI Decision-Making

Accountability in AI-generated decisions is a multifaceted challenge that underscores the ethical obligations developers bear. The responsibility of designers and developers of AI technologies extends far beyond mere technical prowess; it involves a conscientious commitment to creating systems that operate fairly, transparently, and without bias. Developers must tackle these obligations by embedding ethical considerations into the design and deployment stages of AI systems. This means conducting thorough impact assessments before deploying technologies to foresee potential adverse effects on individuals and communities. Such preemptive measures are crucial to mitigate any issues emerging later, thereby nurturing trust among users.

AI-driven decisions have a profound impact on individuals' lives, shaping public perceptions and trust in technology. For instance, consider AI applications in healthcare, where algorithms are used for diagnosing diseases or recommending treatments. A flawed decision could lead to misdiagnosis, affecting patient safety and confidence in medical AI solutions. Similarly, in financial services, AI models are often employed to determine creditworthiness. Bias in these systems can lead to unfair lending practices, harming marginalized groups and eroding trust in digital financial solutions. Public awareness of these nuances can either bolster or diminish trust in AI applications, emphasizing the need for responsible AI development.

Unfortunately, current legal frameworks often fall short when addressing AI accountability. Many existing regulations were not designed with modern AI capabilities in mind, resulting in gaps that fail to address the unique challenges posed by rapid technological advancements. This inadequacy highlights an imperative for new legislative measures that explicitly delineate roles and responsibilities across the AI landscape, from developers to end-users. By doing so, we can create a robust regulatory environment that ensures accountability at every stage of the AI lifecycle.

To overcome these regulatory shortcomings, proposed frameworks suggest new ways of tracking decisions across human and machine components, ensuring developers do not evade responsibility even amid technological ambiguities. One procedural framework includes conducting impact assessments, continuous risk monitoring, incident response planning, and mapping out accountability. These steps aim to operationalize accountability, providing developers and business leaders with structured approaches to managing AI risks—a vital step toward societal benefit. In parallel, an oversight framework advocates establishing ethics boards and implementing regular algorithmic audits to ensure transparency and fairness, encouraging community involvement.

Building public trust requires engaging communities in ongoing discussions about AI ethics. Community engagement fosters transparency and inclusivity, allowing those affected by AI systems to voice their concerns and offer insights during the design and implementation processes. Open dialogues between tech developers and the public can demystify AI technologies, highlighting both their potentials and pitfalls, while empowering communities to partake in shaping ethical guidelines for future developments. By involving diverse voices, especially those from vulnerable and underserved populations, developers gain broader perspectives critical in anticipating and addressing ethical dilemmas in AI deployment.

10.4 Mitigation Strategies for Bias

In the realm of artificial intelligence (AI), reducing bias within systems is a critical challenge that demands thoughtful strategies. Bias in AI can have significant ethical and practical consequences, leading to unjust outcomes and eroding public trust. To address this issue, several techniques can be employed to mitigate bias, ensuring AI systems are fair and equitable.

Continuous evaluation and improvement of AI models are fundamental. This involves regular assessments to detect and correct biases as they arise. By continuously monitoring AI systems, developers can identify patterns that may lead to skewed decisions or unfair treatment of certain groups. Regular audits, both internal and by independent third parties, play a vital role in this process, ensuring objectivity in identifying and correcting biases. Accountability mechanisms such as these ensure that any biases identified are addressed promptly, maintaining the system's integrity and fairness.

A collaborative approach involving ethicists and community leaders is essential for a comprehensive understanding of bias issues. Ethicists provide insights into how biases may manifest in AI systems, while community leaders offer perspectives on the potential impacts on various demographic groups. Engaging with stakeholders from diverse backgrounds ensures that multiple viewpoints are considered, helping to identify biases that may not be apparent from a purely technical standpoint. This collaboration fosters more inclusive and equitable solutions by integrating ethical considerations and community insights into the design and deployment of AI systems.

Transparency in performance metrics is another crucial aspect of reducing bias. When organizations are transparent about the metrics used to evaluate AI systems, it drives accountability and fairness. It allows stakeholders to understand how decisions are made and what factors influence those decisions. Transparency reports detailing an AI system's performance, the data used, and the measures taken to mitigate bias contribute to building trust among users and stakeholders. This openness helps to demystify the often-complex processes behind AI decision-making, making them more comprehensible and allowing for greater scrutiny and input from diverse sources.

Success stories highlight the potential of AI systems when bias mitigation strategies are applied effectively. These examples demonstrate the transformative power of fair AI systems that enhance decision-making processes across various fields. For instance, some companies have successfully implemented diverse data collection practices that reduce bias in their AI predictions, leading to fairer outcomes and improved customer satisfaction. Such stories serve as benchmarks for other organizations, illustrating the benefits of investing in bias reduction techniques and encouraging widespread adoption of these practices.

It is crucial to note that governance frameworks play an instrumental role in supporting the mentioned strategies. Effective governance involves developing clear guidelines and involving a diverse range of stakeholders throughout the AI life-cycle. For example, data collection guidelines should mandate using diverse and representative datasets to train AI models, thus reducing the risk of bias from the outset. Additionally, algorithm development guidelines should ensure that fairness and equity are prioritized, incorporating techniques designed to detect and correct biases during the early stages of AI model development. By embedding fairness into the foundation of AI systems, organizations can create more robust and trustworthy technologies.

Moreover, regular stakeholder consultations and workshops can facilitate ongoing dialogue and collaboration between technologists, ethicists, community representatives, and other key players. These interactions help maintain a constant flow of ideas and feedback, promoting continuous improvement in AI systems. They also ensure that AI development aligns with societal values and addresses the needs and concerns of affected communities, particularly those most vulnerable to bias.

10.5 Legal Considerations in AI Ethics

Emerging technologies like Artificial Intelligence (AI) bring not only innovative benefits but also complex ethical issues, especially in terms of data privacy and accountability. Understanding the laws and regulations governing AI ethics is essential to navigate these challenges effectively. This section delves into significant laws impacting AI ethics like the General Data Protection Regulation (GDPR), other global regulations, ongoing debates about evolving legal standards, and real-world case studies revealing the complexities of assigning legal responsibility for AI decisions.

The General Data Protection Regulation (GDPR) stands out as a landmark legislation enacted by the European Union to protect individual privacy and govern data use. Under GDPR, individuals possess extensive rights over their personal data, such as the right to access, rectify, or even erase their information. These rights place constraints on how businesses and developers can process data, mandating them to secure explicit consent from users before collecting or using personal data. For users, this regulation translates into a greater control over their personal information, promoting increased transparency and trust between consumers and organizations employing AI technologies. By emphasizing the necessity for compliance with strict data protection principles, GDPR serves as a model that many countries aim to emulate or adapt to fit within their national contexts.

Beyond GDPR, similar laws across the globe are beginning to take shape. The California Consumer Privacy Act (CCPA) in the United States, for example, extends comparable protections to consumers within California. While offering less comprehensive coverage compared to GDPR, CCPA represents a significant step forward in American data privacy law. Meanwhile, other regions such as China are formulating their own frameworks for regulating AI ethics, which may prioritize government oversight and data sovereignty more heavily. These developing regulations highlight both similarities and contrasts shaped by cultural, economic, and political factors inherent to different jurisdictions.

As AI continues to evolve rapidly, so too do the legal landscapes surrounding its ethical use. New debates regarding appropriate regulatory measures arise frequently. Calls for international cooperation suggest that while local laws like GDPR and CCPA provide groundwork, there remains an urgent need for unified, global standards. Stakeholders across industries argue whether existing laws suffice to regulate cutting-edge advancements or if entirely new mechanisms are required to keep pace with technological change. Concurrently, policymakers face mounting pressure to balance innovation with ethical safeguards, ensuring AI applications do not infringe upon basic human rights.

Ensuring adherence to current laws builds foundational trust with users by underscoring companies' commitment to respecting individuals' privacy. Compliance is more than just meeting legal obligations; it embodies corporate responsibility towards fair practices in using consumer data. For businesses, incorporating stringent data governance protocols within operational procedures exemplifies ethical engagement while presenting opportunities to cultivate loyalty among tech-savvy consumers. Implementing regular audits to monitor compliance further minimizes risks related to breaches, showcasing transparency and accountability in managing sensitive information.

While regulations guide ethical considerations theoretically, practical application presents its set of challenges. Case studies offer illuminating examples, providing insights into when established procedures both succeed and encounter obstacles. Consider the scenario where autonomous vehicles interact in public spaces. Determining accountability becomes perplexing as machine learning algorithms operate vehicles, requiring human intervention only occasionally. Should an accident occur, attributing responsibility proves intricate—was it programmer error, algorithm malfunction, or sensor failure? These nuances underscore why dissecting real-life instances carries significant educational value in understanding how legal doctrines apply within multifaceted AI environments.

Moreover, exploring situations involving healthcare illustrates another layer of complexity faced when deciphering ethical dilemmas. Suppose an AI system predicts patient treatment plans inaccurately due to bias embedded during training data selection. Assigning blame raises profound questions: who bears ultimate responsibility—the hospital deploying faulty AI systems without rigorous validation, or developers overlooking diverse testing methodologies? This complexity highlights the significance of scrutinizing assumptions underpinning decisions made within opaque systems.

10.6 Final Insights

In this chapter, we've explored the significant ethical dilemmas that AI systems present, focusing primarily on bias and fairness. Bias in AI can perpetuate existing prejudices, leading to unfair treatment of marginalized communities in critical areas such as hiring, finance, and criminal justice. Data fed into AI often mirrors societal biases, making it essential to use diverse datasets and develop standard metrics for evaluating fairness in AI systems. Addressing these concerns not only enhances fairness but also builds trust among users by promoting transparency and accountability. Business professionals and developers are called upon to act ethically, ensuring AI fosters societal benefit rather than reinforcing inequalities.

Additionally, we delved into privacy concerns surrounding AI data and the importance of accountability in AI decision-making. As AI systems handle vast amounts of personal data, robust security measures become paramount to prevent breaches and misuse. Legal considerations like GDPR and CCPA provide frameworks for safeguarding privacy, urging businesses to remain compliant while maintaining the individuals' rights. Understanding these legal and ethical dimensions is crucial for business leaders, students, and tech enthusiasts alike, as they navigate the complexities of AI ethics. By fostering a culture of ethical awareness and responsibility, stakeholders can contribute to shaping a future where AI serves humanity equitably and responsibly.

Chapter 11: AI and Society: Broad Impacts and Implications

T he integration of artificial intelligence (AI) into our daily lives has sparked a transformation in how society interacts and communicates. As AI technologies are increasingly woven into social media platforms, dating apps, and professional environments, the way we connect with each other is undergoing profound changes. These technologies not only influence personal relationships but also reshape professional communication, leading to new dynamics in human interaction.

This chapter dives into the diverse impacts of AI on societal interactions and communication by examining various domains where these technologies play a crucial role. You'll explore how AI shapes content on social media and influences user engagement, potentially creating echo chambers that can lead to increased polarization. Additionally, we'll delve into the intricacies of AI-driven dating algorithms and their effects on romantic relationship dynamics. In professional settings, AI contributes to communication efficiencies, though it comes with challenges related to maintaining personalized interactions. Lastly, we'll discuss AI's pivotal role in crisis management and the associated risks of misinformation dissemination. Through this exploration, you'll gain insights into both the benefits and potential drawbacks of AI as it reshapes how we communicate and interact within society.

11.1 Impact on Social Interactions and Communication

Artificial Intelligence (AI) has deeply embedded itself into the fabric of modern communication and interaction, significantly altering how people engage with one another. As AI technologies permeate social media platforms, dating apps, professional environments, and even crisis management systems, their influence on human communication becomes increasingly evident.

In the realm of social media, AI algorithms curate content feeds designed to maximize user engagement by tailoring the displayed information according to perceived user interests. While this personalized approach can enhance user experience by delivering content that aligns with individual preferences, it also inadvertently fosters the formation of echo chambers. By continuously exposing users to similar ideas and perspectives, these algorithms can limit exposure to diverse viewpoints, skewing public discourse towards more homogeneous narratives. This phenomenon raises concerns about the potential for increased polarization, as people may become less likely to encounter or engage with differing opinions. A study by Cinelli et al highlights how these echo chambers develop through homophily in interaction networks, where like-minded individuals reinforce one another's beliefs, further entrenching

167

divisions within society.

The impact of AI extends beyond social media into the domain of personal relationships, particularly through the use of AI-driven dating algorithms. These algorithms utilize vast amounts of data to match individuals based on compatibility factors determined by user activity, preferences, and profiles. While they streamline the process of finding potential partners, they also shape romantic relationship dynamics by setting specific expectations. Users may begin to rely heavily on algorithm-generated matches, potentially narrowing their understanding of compatibility and influencing their interactions and decisions in forming relationships. The delicate balance between algorithmic efficiency and genuine human connection is an ongoing conversation in the context of romance.

Professionally, AI facilitates communication efficiencies through automated messaging systems, which are becoming standard in many workplaces. The automation of routine tasks, such as scheduling meetings, managing emails, or responding to common queries, allows professionals to allocate more time to critical tasks that require human insight and creativity. However, there is a caveat. The reliance on AI for professional communication introduces challenges, especially when automated messages replace personalized interactions. The absence of nuanced human touch in communication may lead to misunderstandings or misinterpretations, as AI struggles to grasp the subtleties of context and sentiment intrinsic to human language. Thus, while task management is streamlined, ensuring clarity and maintaining interpersonal rapport presents new challenges.

In times of crisis, AI plays an indispensable role in rapidly disseminating information, enabling swift responses to urgent situations. For instance, during natural disasters or public health emergencies, AI systems can analyze vast datasets to provide real-time updates and alerts, helping coordinate relief efforts and inform the public. However, the speed and scale at which AI operates bring forth issues of misinformation dissemination. The same algorithms that allow rapid information spread can also amplify false or misleading information, potentially exacerbating panic or leading to misguided actions. Transparency in algorithmic processes and source verification is crucial to mitigate misinformation risks and maintain public trust in AI-driven communications.

Across these domains, the implications of AI on human interaction call for a nuanced understanding of the technology's benefits and drawbacks. While AI offers enhanced personalization and efficiency, it simultaneously presents challenges that necessitate careful consideration and strategic implementation. Promoting digital literacy and fostering awareness of AI's influence on communication can empower individuals to navigate these changes thoughtfully and responsibly. Encouraging open dialogue about the ethical use of AI technologies and cultivating critical thinking skills are essential steps toward harnessing AI's potential while safeguarding meaningful human connections.

11.2 AI's Influence on Economic Structures

Artificial intelligence (AI) is reshaping our economic landscape and job markets at an unprecedented pace. Its transformative effects are particularly evident in how automation, spurred by AI, is altering job dynamics across the globe. For many industries, automation promises great efficiency, yet it also poses significant challenges for workers whose tasks can be automated.

Automation threatens certain jobs, especially those involving repetitive and routine tasks. From assembly lines to customer service centers, AI technologies now perform roles that were once human-dominated. As automation increases productivity, it also alters wage structures, impacting economic systems. For instance, industries reliant on manual labor may see a reduction in employment opportunities, potentially leading to wage stagnation or decline in these sectors. Meanwhile, jobs requiring advanced technical skills could experience a surge in demand and wages, contributing to a growing skills gap in the workforce. This scenario necessitates comprehensive workforce adaptation strategies, crucial to equipping individuals with skills that meet the evolving market demands. Upskilling and reskilling initiatives become essential as they help workers transition into new roles that AI cannot fully replicate, thus maintaining their employability.

AI's impact is not just limited to individual industries; it also plays a key role in wealth distribution within economies. AI-centric corporations, often pioneers in adopting these technologies, risk concentrating significant wealth and power.

Such concentration challenges equitable economic distribution, posing socio-economic risks. Without appropriate policy interventions, these corporations could widen the economic disparities as they dominate industries with high entry barriers for smaller firms. Policymakers must consider frameworks that promote diversity and inclusivity, ensuring smaller players have fair opportunities to compete.

Supply chains across the globe are also undergoing transformation due to AI. By optimizing logistics, production schedules, and inventory management, AI streamlines operations, reducing costs and enhancing efficiency. Automated production processes are revolutionizing global trade dynamics, allowing companies to respond rapidly to market changes and consumer demands. However, these efficiencies might lead to shifts in labor markets, particularly affecting regions heavily dependent on manufacturing jobs. Workers in these areas face the threat of job displacement, demanding strategic interventions from governments to support affected communities through training and development programs.

Furthermore, AI fuels innovation among startups, disrupting traditional business models and shifting investment landscapes. These startups leverage AI to challenge established norms, introducing products and services that redefine consumer expectations and industry standards. Consequently, this drives investment trends towards ventures that prioritize AI integration, reflecting a broader venture capital shift favoring technological advancement. Startups that adeptly harness AI technologies position themselves as attractive prospects for investors keen on supporting cutting-edge development.

11.3 Global Implications of AI Development

The rapid advancements in artificial intelligence (AI) are re-shaping global dynamics, with profound implications for national security and geopolitical strategy. Nations across the world are investing heavily in AI technologies, recognizing their potential to revolutionize defense capabilities and strategic positioning. For instance, countries like the United States and China are at the forefront of this race, viewing AI as a critical component in maintaining or achieving military superiority. The expansion of AI in defense sectors not only strengthens individual nations but also influences international power structures, fostering both competition and opportunities for cooperation.

AI's role in national security extends beyond military applications, impacting geopolitical strategies profoundly. With AI-driven systems, governments can enhance surveillance, intelligence gathering, and decision-making processes, creating a new frontier in security strategies. However, this technological leap also raises concerns about an arms race, where nations might prioritize AI development over diplomatic engagements, potentially leading to tensions and conflicts. To mitigate these risks, it is crucial for countries to engage in collaborative dialogues, establish common ground, and explore mutually beneficial agreements that leverage AI's capabilities while promoting peace and stability on a global scale.

Another significant challenge is the varying standards of AI governance across different nations. This disparity can impede global collaboration when regulatory discrepancies arise.

Countries often develop their own AI policies, reflecting local values, priorities, and ethical considerations, which may not align with those of others. These differences can hinder cross-border AI collaborations, as organizations and developers need to navigate a complex maze of regulations that vary widely from one jurisdiction to another. This inconsistency complicates efforts to create unified AI governance frameworks, essential for managing the technology's global impact.

To overcome these hurdles, international cooperation in establishing standardized AI governance should be prioritized. Multilateral organizations and forums can play pivotal roles in harmonizing regulations and creating guidelines that respect cultural diversity while ensuring AI's responsible use. Collaborative efforts could focus on developing universally accepted principles, such as transparency, accountability, and privacy protection, which form the foundation of trustworthy AI systems. By aligning AI governance standards, nations can facilitate smoother global integration and ensure that benefits are shared equitably among all stakeholders.

The influence of AI extends into cultural realms, where local contexts significantly shape its applications. In some regions, AI-driven technologies can enhance cultural exchange by breaking language barriers, improving access to diverse content, and preserving cultural heritage through digital means. For instance, AI-powered translation tools enable seamless communication across languages, fostering understanding and appreciation of different cultures. Similarly, digitization projects supported by AI can document and revive endangered languages, ensuring their preservation for future generations.

Conversely, there is a risk of cultural dominance, where technologically advanced nations or corporations imprint their values and practices on less developed regions. This cultural hegemony can lead to homogenization, eroding local traditions and identities. Therefore, it is imperative to recognize and respect the cultural nuances present in AI deployment. Encouraging the development of AI applications tailored to local needs and contexts can promote cultural diversity and empower communities to harness AI for their benefits.

Aligning AI advancements with sustainability goals is another critical consideration. As the technology evolves, so do concerns over its environmental footprint. The energy demand of AI models, particularly those requiring substantial computational power, poses challenges to sustainability. To address this, balancing AI's benefits against environmental costs is crucial. Researchers and policymakers must collaborate to design energy-efficient algorithms and encourage green computing practices that reduce carbon emissions and resource consumption.

Moreover, integrating sustainable practices into AI development aligns with the broader objective of achieving the United Nations' Sustainable Development Goals (SDGs). AI can be leveraged to tackle pressing issues such as climate change, resource management, and conservation efforts. For example, AI-driven predictive models can optimize energy consumption in smart grids, enhance precision in agriculture, and monitor ecological patterns for better conservation strategies. By focusing on sustainability, nations can ensure that AI not only drives technological progress but also contributes positively to global well-being and environmental stewardship.

11.4 Economic Inequality and AI

Artificial intelligence (AI) has the potential to dramatically reshape the global economy, raising important questions about its role in either exacerbating or alleviating economic disparity. As AI technologies continue to advance and proliferate, there are mounting concerns about the concentration of wealth among AI-dominant corporations and whether these entities may increase economic inequality without implementing inclusive practices.

The rise of AI has enabled companies that dominate this space to accumulate significant wealth and influence. These corporations often benefit from substantial investments in AI research and development, leading to a competitive edge that can outpace other firms. However, when these technological advancements are not accompanied by inclusive business strategies, the result can be a greater concentration of economic power within a small cluster of entities. This accumulation of power can potentially widen the gap between the wealthy and less affluent populations, creating an uneven distribution of resources and opportunities.

One way to mitigate these disparities is through democratizing access to high-quality education and resources via AI. By providing equal access to AI-driven educational tools and learning platforms, individuals from diverse socioeconomic backgrounds can gain skills and knowledge critical for succeeding in a technology-driven future. Innovative programs leveraging AI to personalize education and offer real-time feedback have already begun to close gaps in educational attainment. This democratization can create more equitable opportunities, empowering a broad range of people to participate fully in the digital economy.

Furthermore, investing in equitable AI deployment is crucial for ensuring fairer wealth distribution within societies. Equitable deployment means that AI technologies should not only serve the interests of large corporations but also address societal needs, such as improving healthcare, enhancing infrastructure, and supporting small businesses. Governments and companies can play a pivotal role by committing to investments in areas where AI can have widespread social benefits, particularly in underserved communities. For instance, deploying AI in local public services can enhance efficiency and accessibility, ensuring that all citizens benefit from technological progress.

Another significant aspect to consider is the role of technological collaborations in fostering balanced economic relations globally. As AI becomes a central component of international trade, new trade agreements will be necessary to ensure that economic benefits are shared equitably among participating nations. Collaborative partnerships between countries can facilitate the exchange of AI-related expertise and resources, allowing nations with varying levels of technological infrastructure to advance collectively. Such collaborations could promote innovation while preventing economic divides that might arise from disparate access to AI capabilities.

For example, nurturing partnerships between technologically

advanced countries and those still developing their AI infrastructure could lead to joint ventures and collaborative R&D
projects. By sharing insights and resources, countries can
achieve mutual growth and prevent the deepening of economic
disparities on a global scale. Additionally, establishing fair
trade agreements that account for AI's unique attributes can
help regulate the flow of AI technologies across borders, encouraging a level playing field for all participants.

In light of these considerations, policymakers and stakeholders must take proactive measures to navigate the complex
landscape of AI-driven economic change. Addressing the
risks associated with wealth concentration requires thoughtful
legislation and corporate governance focused on transparency
and accountability. Ensuring that AI technologies are deployed
ethically and inclusively will contribute significantly to reducing economic inequality and fostering a fairer distribution of
resources.

Moreover, prioritizing investment in education and workforce development can prepare individuals for an AI-driven
economy. Implementing programs that emphasize reskilling
and upskilling can equip workers with the necessary tools to
adapt to evolving job markets. As AI continues to transform
industries, providing accessible training resources becomes
essential to avoid leaving large segments of the population
behind.

Ultimately, the impact of AI on economic disparity hinges on
the policy choices made today. If appropriately harnessed,
AI holds the promise of serving social good by lifting living

standards and bridging economic gaps. By adopting inclusive practices, promoting equitable deployment, and fostering international cooperation, societies can unlock AI's full potential while mitigating the risks of economic inequality.

11.5 Entrepreneurship and Innovation Through AI

Artificial intelligence (AI) is an incredible force reshaping how startups are conceived and operated, offering new pathways for entrepreneurs to explore. At the heart of this revolution is the way AI technologies challenge existing market conventions, driving advancement across various industries. Startups are leveraging AI to innovate by introducing novel products and services that disrupt traditional business models. This process often involves creating solutions that address specific industry pain points that were previously unmanageable with conventional methods. For example, AI-powered tools can optimize processes in real-time or predict market trends with greater accuracy, granting businesses a competitive edge.

The advancements brought by AI startups have not gone unnoticed. Investors are increasingly drawn to AI-driven businesses due to their potential to upend industries while offering significant growth opportunities. This trend signifies a growing recognition of AI technologies' disruptive potential and the transformative impact they can have on global markets. According to recent data, there's been a surge in venture capital flowing into AI sectors, highlighting how investors are betting big on AI's future to yield substantial returns. Such investments are not just about capital but also about trust in AI's ability to innovate effectively.

Emerging entrepreneurial strategies further underscore the transformative nature of AI. Traditional business approaches are being redefined as companies integrate AI into their frameworks. AI allows businesses to operate more efficiently and create value in unprecedented ways, whether through automating mundane tasks or devising entirely new business models. The development of agile methodologies that incorporate AI solutions has become essential for startups aiming to thrive in today's fast-paced environment. These strategies often rely on interdisciplinary collaboration, where AI experts join forces with industry specialists to develop comprehensive solutions that can cater to diverse market needs.

In addition to operational changes, venture capitalists (VCs) are significantly altering their investment strategies to align with the potential offered by AI innovations. This shift reflects a broader adaptation within the investment community, driven by the realization that supporting cutting-edge AI development can lead to groundbreaking advancements and lucrative outcomes. Venture capital firms are now prioritizing AI startups over traditional ventures, seeing them as vehicles capable of leading the next wave of technological evolution. This focus on AI-centric investments is reshaping funding landscapes, ensuring that resources flow toward initiatives with the highest promise of disrupting and enhancing existing markets.

Moreover, the role of VCs extends beyond mere funding. They provide mentorship and strategic guidance that helps AI startups navigate the complexities of growth and market entry. With their profound understanding of industry dynamics and extensive networks, VCs are well-positioned to assist startups in building robust business models and forming strategic partnerships necessary for scaling operations. This collaborative dynamic between startups and VCs underscores the symbiotic relationship required to foster innovation and push the boundaries of what AI can achieve.

The increasing importance of ethical considerations also plays a vital role in the AI entrepreneurial landscape. Startups are urged to prioritize ethical AI integration, ensuring that technologies are deployed responsibly and transparently. By doing so, they build trust with consumers and stakeholders, which is crucial for sustainable growth. Ethical practices help mitigate risks associated with biases and other unintended consequences that may arise from AI deployment. Investors and entrepreneurs alike recognize that maintaining transparency and accountability is pivotal in shaping positive public perception and embracing the full potential of AI.

11.6 Final Insights

The exploration of AI's impact on societal interactions reveals profound changes in the way we communicate and connect with one another. From social media to personal relationships, AI technologies are reshaping how we engage, often enhancing efficiency but sometimes at the cost of diversity and deeper human connections. In social media, algorithms tailor content to align with user preferences, creating echo chambers that can limit exposure to differing ideas. Personal relationships, particularly in dating, witness a shift as AI-driven matches set expectations and influence dynamics. Meanwhile, in professional settings, AI automates routine tasks, freeing time for creative endeavors but necessitating careful attention to maintain meaningful personal interactions. During crises, AI accelerates communication, yet it requires vigilance to prevent misinformation spread. As we navigate these shifts, promoting awareness and digital literacy becomes vital, empowering individuals to thoughtfully adapt to AI's influence.

On the economic front, AI presents both opportunities and challenges, impacting job markets, wealth distribution, and global trade. Automation enhances productivity but risks job displacement, especially in repetitive roles, while increasing demand for technical skills, prompting workforce adaptation through upskilling initiatives. Wealth distribution faces the risk of concentration among dominant AI-centric corporations, urging policy frameworks to ensure equitable opportunities. Furthermore, AI optimizes supply chains and fuels innovation, driving startups to disrupt traditional business models. These transformations highlight the need for sustainable practices to balance environmental impacts, aligning AI advancements with global well-being goals. By harnessing AI responsibly and inclusively, societies can leverage its potential to bridge economic gaps and foster innovation across industries, ensuring progress benefits everyone.

Chapter 12: Future Trends: The Road Ahead for AI

E xploring future trends in artificial intelligence (AI) offers a fascinating glimpse into the technological advancements that lie ahead. As AI continues to evolve, it is reshaping various landscapes, from healthcare to finance, signaling a paradigm shift in how we perceive and utilize technology. The potential of AI extends far beyond its current capabilities, promising innovations that could redefine industries and transform everyday life. This journey into future possibilities invites us to imagine a world where technology and human ingenuity converge seamlessly, opening doors to new opportunities and challenges.

In this chapter, we delve into the intriguing developments anticipated in AI's future trajectory. We will examine emerging technologies such as explainable AI, which aims to increase transparency and trust by shedding light on AI decision-making processes. Concepts like federated learning promise to revolutionize data privacy while enhancing AI model accuracy across decentralized networks. By blending neural and symbolic reasoning, neurosymbolic AI offers fresh avenues for cognitive technologies, potentially transforming fields requiring complex problem-solving. We'll also explore quantum AI's potential to enhance computational capacities and examine its implications across different sectors. Together, these advancements paint a picture of the road ahead, highlighting the transformative impact AI could have on industries and our daily lives.

12.1 Advancements in AI Research

Artificial intelligence (AI) has rapidly advanced in recent years, bringing both excitement and challenges to different industries. One of the latest developments is Explainable AI, which aims to enhance the transparency of AI systems. In traditional AI, outcomes and decisions are often a "black box," meaning users do not fully understand how conclusions are reached. Explainable AI seeks to address this issue by providing clear explanations of how AI models arrive at specific outcomes. By improving transparency, Explainable AI fosters greater trust between humans and AI systems, facilitating more effective collaboration. For instance, in healthcare, doctors can better interpret AI-generated diagnostics when they understand the rationale behind them. This leads to improved decision-making and patient care.

Another breakthrough in AI is Federated Learning, which introduces a novel way of training AI models across decentralized data sources. Traditional models require data to be centralized for processing, which raises privacy concerns. Federated Learning allows AI systems to learn from diverse datasets without necessitating the transfer of local data to a central server. This decentralized approach preserves user privacy while still enabling the creation of robust and accurate models. Federated Learning is particularly beneficial in sectors like finance and healthcare, where sensitive data is involved. As privacy becomes increasingly important, this method offers an innovative solution that balances data utility with security.

Neurosymbolic AI represents another exciting development. It blends neural networks, known for handling large volumes of unstructured data, with symbolic reasoning, which excels at logical tasks. This combination allows AI systems to perform complex reasoning that mimics human thought processes. For example, while neural networks might be excellent at recognizing patterns in images, incorporating symbolic reasoning enables the machine to understand and articulate why those patterns exist. Such capabilities are crucial in domains requiring sophisticated problem-solving abilities, like legal analysis or scientific research. Neurosymbolic AI could revolutionize fields where understanding nuances and making inferences from vast amounts of data are critical.

Quantum AI stands on the frontier of AI advancements, leveraging the unique properties of quantum computing to push boundaries in processing speeds and capabilities. Traditional computers process information in bits, as 0s or 1s, but quantum computers use qubits, which can represent both values simultaneously thanks to superposition. This allows quantum computers to perform computations far faster than classical machines. When applied to AI, this could mean processing immense datasets or solving complex optimization problems that are currently daunting. For instance, in pharmaceuticals, Quantum AI might expedite drug discovery by rapidly modeling molecular interactions. While practical quantum computing remains a work in progress, its potential impact on AI is vast, promising breakthroughs across numerous sectors.

The integration of these concepts presents a transformative trajectory for AI, influencing various industries in unprecedented ways. Explainable AI could lead to more accountable and ethical AI applications, especially in regulated environments like finance, where decision transparency is legally required. Federated Learning's ability to handle localized data training will only grow more essential as data privacy regulations tighten globally. Meanwhile, the blend of neural and symbolic methodologies in Neurosymbolic AI might pave new paths in cognitive technologies, allowing for AI systems that can not only solve problems but also understand the underlying principles driving them.

Moreover, Quantum AI holds the promise of reshaping sectors reliant on heavy computational tasks. From climate modeling, which requires processing vast environmental datasets, to cryptography, where secure communication methods can benefit from the complexity offered by quantum computations, the possibilities are extensive. The ongoing research into developing stable and scalable quantum systems means that the convergence of quantum technologies with AI is likely to become a cornerstone in future technological landscapes.

12.2 AI in Environmental Sustainability

Artificial Intelligence (AI) is increasingly seen as a pivotal player in tackling some of the most pressing environmental challenges we face. By leveraging data and computational power, AI can offer solutions that are both innovative and efficient, addressing issues across various sectors such as resource management, climate science, biodiversity conservation, and pollution control.

Let's begin with how AI contributes to smart resource management. The traditional methods of managing resources like energy and water have often led to inefficiencies and significant wastage. Here, AI comes into play by optimizing these processes. Using sophisticated algorithms, AI systems can predict consumption patterns and adjust resource distribution accordingly. For example, smart grids powered by AI can manage electricity flow more effectively, reducing losses and balancing supply and demand dynamically. Similarly, AI-driven systems in agriculture could determine optimal watering schedules for crops, conserving water while maximizing yield. This precision in resource usage not only cuts down on waste but also significantly reduces emissions linked to excessive energy production and water misuse. A practical guideline here would be integrating AI systems into existing resource infrastructures to monitor and adjust usage in real-time.

Climate modeling is another area where AI shows immense potential. Accurate climate predictions are crucial for preparing and mitigating natural disasters. AI enhances climate models by processing vast amounts of meteorological data much faster than traditional methods, improving the accuracy of weather predictions. For instance, AI can analyze historical climate data alongside current measurements to forecast future weather patterns with higher precision. This information aids governments and agencies in crafting strategies for disaster preparedness and response, potentially saving lives and reducing economic losses caused by unforeseen weather events and calamities. Such mitigation strategies become easier to implement when equipped with AI-generated insights, allowing timely evacuations and targeted resource allocation.

When it comes to biodiversity monitoring, AI presents new opportunities to protect wildlife and their habitats. Traditional methods of monitoring species and ecosystems are labor-intensive and often limited in scope. AI technology can transform this by utilizing drones, satellite images, and sensor networks to provide continuous and comprehensive surveillance of diverse environments. Algorithms can process these massive datasets to detect changes in biodiversity, such as declining animal populations or habitat destruction, which might otherwise go unnoticed until it's too late. Real-time tracking enabled by AI allows conservationists to take immediate action, such as relocating threatened species or restoring compromised habitats. With this information at hand, policymakers can design better conservation strategies that are responsive and data-driven.

Pollution control is integral to maintaining a healthy planet, and here's where AI shines once again. Identifying pollution sources is often the first step in managing environmental quality, yet it remains challenging due to the complexity and interconnectivity of modern industrial activities. AI can assist by analyzing complex data sets from environmental sensors, detecting patterns of pollution and pinpointing their origins. For example, AI systems can distinguish between different emission sources, whether from vehicles, factories, or natural occurrences, enabling more targeted regulatory efforts. Furthermore, AI can simulate various policy scenarios, predicting outcomes and helping policymakers choose the most effective measures for reducing pollutants. This method not just controls pollution levels but also guides the creation of robust and adaptable policy frameworks tailored to specific regional needs.

In each of these areas, there is an underlying guideline: the integration of AI into environmental management must be systematic and thoughtful. It requires collaboration between technologists, policymakers, and community stakeholders to ensure that the data used is reliable and ethically sourced and that the AI models are transparent and unbiased. Transitioning to AI-driven environmental management will call for investments in infrastructure and training, equipping individuals with the skills needed to harness AI technologies effectively.

12.3 Futuristic AI Concepts and Technologies

As we venture into a future where artificial intelligence (AI) continues to evolve at an extraordinary pace, one of the most captivating possibilities is the development of Artificial General Intelligence (AGI). Unlike narrow AI, which excels in specific tasks such as language translation or image recognition, AGI aims to equip machines with cognitive abilities comparable to humans. This includes understanding, learning, and applying intelligence across various complex tasks without explicit programming. Imagine machines capable of solving diverse problems and generating creative solutions, similar to human capability.

The realization of AGI could fundamentally redefine industries and drive innovation in unprecedented ways. For instance, in healthcare, AGI could enhance diagnostics by analyzing medical records, symptoms, and scientific research to recommend tailored treatments. In education, it may offer personalized learning experiences for students, adapting teaching methods to individual needs, thereby revolutionizing the educational landscape. Moreover, AGI's potential to augment creativity might lead to groundbreaking advancements in fields like art, music, and literature, where machines collaborate with humans to produce novel works.

Another transformative trend involves merging synthetic biology with AI. Through this synergy, we are witnessing remarkable advancements in medicine, agriculture, and environmental protection. At its core, synthetic biology involves designing and constructing new biological parts, devices, and systems— often aided by AI's predictive capabilities. For example, AI can analyze vast datasets from genetic research, accelerating the development of therapies for diseases such as cancer and genetic disorders. In agriculture, AI-driven synthetic biology might lead to crops that exhibit increased resilience to pests and climate variations, boosting food security. Environmental sustainability, too, benefits from this collaboration; engineered microorganisms could be used to clean up pollutants, offering innovative solutions for environmental challenges.

One of the forefront developments in redefining our interaction with machines is the advent of brain-computer interfaces (BCIs). These interfaces create direct communication pathways between the human brain and external devices powered by AI. Such technology holds immense potential in enhancing human capabilities. For individuals with disabilities, BCIs could restore motor functions or facilitate communication by translating neural activity into commands for prosthetic limbs or speech synthesizers. However, as promising as BCIs are, they raise significant ethical considerations regarding privacy and consent, given their ability to access and interpret thoughts. Ensuring responsible usage and clear ethical guidelines will be paramount as this technology progresses.

In parallel, AI-powered decision-making systems are increasingly shaping industries by analyzing vast amounts of data to provide targeted insights. These systems excel in recognizing patterns and trends, enabling businesses to make informed decisions quickly. In finance, for instance, AI algorithms can predict market fluctuations, helping investors optimize portfolios. Retailers use AI to study consumer behavior, optimizing inventory and improving customer experiences. Nonetheless, the deployment of such systems necessitates careful ethical oversight to prevent biases and ensure fairness. As AI becomes integral in decision-making processes, transparency and accountability must be prioritized to maintain trust within society.

The ongoing evolution of these visionary AI technologies underscores the profound impact they have on human-machine interactions. By transforming problem-solving, fostering collaborations across disciplines, and analyzing complex data, AI opens doors to opportunities previously unimaginable. As we navigate this journey, it remains crucial to balance innovation with ethical considerations, ensuring these technologies enhance our world while respecting human values and promoting inclusive progress.

12.4 Emerging Synergies Between AI and Other Technologies

In the rapidly evolving landscape of artificial intelligence, integrating AI with other advanced technologies opens new horizons for innovation and problem-solving. One such integration is with quantum computing, a field set to revolutionize classical computing through its ability to perform complex operations dramatically faster than current systems. The fusion of AI and quantum computing holds potential for breakthroughs in various industries. Quantum computers can handle large datasets and solve optimization problems quickly, making them ideal partners for AI in fields like pharmaceuticals, where they can accelerate drug discovery by evaluating numerous molecules for potential treatments.

Quantum computing's capacity to enhance AI capabilities stems from leveraging quantum mechanics principles using qubits that exist in multiple states simultaneously. This property allows for parallel processing which can significantly boost the efficiency of AI algorithms, leading to more accurate and reliable outputs even with smaller datasets. While this technology is still in developmental stages, its potential applications are vast, ranging from improving financial models to optimizing supply chain logistics.

On another front, the integration of AI with the Internet of Things (IoT) promises to transform urban living through the development of smart cities. IoT devices collect data from various sources—traffic sensors, energy meters, and weather stations—and when combined with AI, provide solutions for improving city infrastructure. For instance, AI-driven data analysis can optimize traffic light controls to reduce congestion or manage energy distribution to ensure efficient consumption during peak hours. These advancements not only enhance everyday convenience but also contribute to sustainability goals by minimizing resource wastage and promoting green energy use.

The relationship between AI and blockchain technology is another exciting frontier. Blockchain's decentralized nature makes it highly secure, providing a perfect platform for AI-driven processes that require transparency and security. For example, in sectors like finance and healthcare where handling sensitive data is critical, integrating AI with blockchain can safeguard information while ensuring that all transactions remain transparent and traceable. Moreover, this combination supports the creation of smart contracts—automated agreements executed under predefined conditions—which streamline operations and reduce the risk of fraud or human error.

A practical application of AI-blockchain synergy can be seen in supply chain management. By implementing blockchain alongside AI, businesses gain a clearer view of every step involved in production and delivery. AI algorithms analyze data across these stages to identify inefficiencies, predict demand, and suggest improvements while blockchain ensures the integrity and security of transaction records, building trust among stakeholders.

Collaborative robotics, or cobots, represent another compelling intersection where AI plays a vital role. Cobots are designed to work alongside humans in industrial settings, enhancing productivity and safety. Unlike traditional robots operating in isolation due to safety concerns, cobots utilize advanced AI to adapt their actions based on real-time input, creating a safer working environment. They assist in tasks like heavy lifting, precision assembly, and quality control, allowing humans to focus on more complex or creative aspects of production. This human-robot partnership not only boosts operational efficiency but also addresses labor shortages, particularly in sectors like manufacturing and healthcare, where automation of routine tasks frees up human resources for critical roles.

In manufacturing, cobots equipped with vision systems use AI to inspect products for defects, ensuring consistent quality throughout mass production processes. In healthcare, robots assist with non-patient facing tasks such as sorting medication, thereby reducing nurses' workloads and allowing them to devote more time to patient care. As these robots become more accessible and communicative, thanks to AI advancements, we can expect unprecedented levels of collaboration between humans and machines.

12.5 Ethical and Societal Implications of Advanced AI

The rapid advancement of artificial intelligence (AI) technologies offers an array of opportunities but also presents significant ethical challenges and societal impacts that demand urgent attention. As AI becomes increasingly integrated into various facets of everyday life, ensuring its development aligns with ethical standards is paramount. Creating fair and unbiased algorithms is essential to maintaining societal trust in AI systems. These algorithms must be developed with a conscious effort to eliminate bias, which can emerge from skewed data sets or pre-existing societal inequities. If left unchecked, biased algorithms can perpetuate discrimination and inequality, ultimately eroding public trust in AI technologies. Developers must approach algorithm design with an acute awareness of these risks, employing diverse datasets and interdisciplinary perspectives to mitigate bias effectively.

In tandem with the ethical development of AI, there is a pressing need for new regulatory frameworks. As AI technologies permeate more aspects of personal and professional life, safeguarding personal autonomy and privacy rights becomes critical. The proliferation of AI has outpaced existing regulatory measures, leaving gaps that could expose individuals to privacy violations and misuse of their data. Comprehensive regulations should focus on defining the acceptable boundaries of AI use, ensuring transparency, and holding organizations accountable for breaches. Such frameworks are pivotal in providing a safety net that protects individuals' rights in an increasingly digital world.

The disruption caused by AI extends beyond ethics and regulation, reaching into the dynamics of job markets and societal structures. With AI taking over tasks traditionally performed by humans, shifts in employment landscapes are inevitable. This transition necessitates policies for workforce adaptation and re-skilling to equip workers with the necessary skills to thrive in an AI-driven environment. By investing in education and training programs that focus on developing complementary skills, society can foster an adaptable workforce capable of working alongside AI. Moreover, the creation of support systems for displaced workers will be crucial to mitigating the adverse effects of automation.

Amid these changes, fostering public discourse around AI is vital. Conversations must emphasize responsible innovation aligned with human values and goals. This dialogue should involve stakeholders from various sectors, including policymakers, technologists, ethicists, and the general public, to ensure a comprehensive understanding of AI's impact. Public engagement in these discussions can help align AI development with societal needs and aspirations, ultimately guiding technology toward enhancing human well-being rather than undermining it.

12.6 Final Insights

As we look towards the future of artificial intelligence, this chapter has explored several exciting advancements and their potential applications across various industries. Explainable

AI, for instance, provides more transparency, allowing users to trust AI-driven outcomes by understanding the decision-making process behind them. Federated Learning addresses privacy concerns by decentralizing data training, which is especially useful in sensitive sectors like healthcare and finance. Then there's Neurosymbolic AI, a promising blend of neural networks and symbolic reasoning, offering enhanced problem-solving capabilities that mimic human logic. Quantum AI pushes the frontiers even further, leveraging quantum computing's speed to tackle complex optimization problems. These innovations are shaping the way industries operate, highlighting the growing importance of AI in our digital age.

This chapter also underscores the transformative synergy between AI and other emerging technologies, such as IoT and blockchain, showing how they can collectively solve complex challenges. The integration of AI with smart city technologies offers solutions for efficient resource management and urban planning. Meanwhile, AI and blockchain partnerships promise secure, transparent processes—crucial for fields managing sensitive data. As these technologies evolve, ethical considerations remain crucial, ensuring developments are fair and accessible to everyone. For beginners, business professionals, students, and entrepreneurs alike, understanding these concepts paves the way for embracing AI's potential to innovate workflows and drive business growth. By keeping an eye on these advancements, we can better prepare for a future where AI is seamlessly intertwined with our daily lives.

Conclusion

I n today's fast-paced, technology-driven world, under-standing artificial intelligence (AI) is not just beneficial; it's essential. Just as learning a new language opens doors to new cultures and perspectives, acquiring knowledge about AI equips you with the tools to better engage with the array of technologies that touch every aspect of our lives. Whether you are a student stepping into the realm of technology, a business professional aiming to innovate, or an entrepreneur seeking to optimize operations, AI serves as a bridge to countless opportunities and efficiencies.

For beginners without any prior technical background, this journey into AI might feel daunting at first. However, breaking down complex concepts into digestible insights can transform this learning curve from an intimidating mountain into a series of manageable steps. Picture it like learning the ropes of cooking; once you grasp the basic techniques, creating intricate dishes becomes exciting rather than overwhelming. Similarly, understanding AI will enable you to critically engage with the evolving technologies around you, making informed choices and participating in conversations that shape the future.

As we integrate AI more deeply into our daily routines, its potential to enhance and streamline our experiences becomes increasingly apparent. From the convenience of smart home devices that adjust lighting and temperature based on your preferences to personalized recommendations that guide your entertainment or shopping choices, AI is transforming how we interact with the world. It's akin to having a personal assistant who learns your likes and dislikes over time, providing support that goes beyond mere novelty to offer genuine improvements to your quality of life. By embracing these advancements, we can optimize our decision-making processes, ultimately leading to richer and more fulfilling daily interactions.

In the business landscape, the transformational power of AI is even more pronounced. As companies adopt AI solutions, they find themselves able to automate repetitive tasks, thus freeing up human resources to focus on strategic objectives. Imagine AI as a trustworthy companion at work, tackling mundane activities while you concentrate on innovation and creative problem-solving. This partnership not only enhances efficiency but also drives customer engagement by improving service delivery and responsiveness. The result? Businesses that leverage AI can potentially unlock unprecedented growth, setting themselves apart in competitive markets through speed, precision, and insight.

However, amid this technological optimism, it's crucial to keep ethical considerations at the forefront. As AI systems become more integrated into society, questions about privacy, bias, and accountability arise. We must approach these challenges thoughtfully and responsibly, ensuring that AI applications benefit everyone fairly and do not perpetuate existing inequalities. Think of this imperative as a collective effort to maintain harmony between progress and principles— much like balancing freedom with responsibility in societal governance. By prioritizing ethical deployment, we align AI developments with values that promote trust and safeguard human dignity.

Looking forward, our relationship with AI will undoubtedly continue to evolve. For students and tech enthusiasts, this means an abundance of career prospects in an industry ripe with innovation. By gaining foundational knowledge of AI today, you position yourself at the cutting edge, ready to explore new frontiers and make meaningful contributions to the field. Meanwhile, entrepreneurs and freelancers stand to gain immensely by incorporating AI into their workflows, achieving business growth through enhanced productivity and innovation. Embracing AI does not replace human ingenuity; rather, it complements it, opening doors to novel possibilities and competitive advantages.

The journey toward AI fluency may begin with curiosity, but it unfolds into a pursuit rich with potential and discovery. Every step taken to understand AI—from grasping core concepts to applying them in real-world scenarios—adds to a collective momentum that propels us toward a more connected, efficient, and innovative future. Imagine holding the key to untapped potential, where the limits of what you can achieve expand exponentially with each new insight acquired.

As you close this chapter on AI basics, remember that the story doesn't end here. The world of AI offers endless chapters waiting to be explored, each offering different applications and insights tailored to your unique interests and goals. Whether you apply this knowledge to enhance personal endeavors, drive business transformation, or embark on new technological ventures, the possibilities are vast and varied.

Ultimately, by understanding and harnessing the power of AI, you're not merely adapting to change—you're becoming an active participant in shaping the technological landscape of tomorrow. With each deliberate choice and innovative application, you contribute to a world where AI functions as an ally, enhancing human capabilities and enriching our shared experiences. Let this be the beginning of an exciting adventure, one where you play a pivotal role in defining how AI will serve as an engine for progress and prosperity across all walks of life.

With these thoughts in mind, take the knowledge you've gained and let it fuel your vision, creativity, and ambition. The horizon is wide open, offering infinite opportunities for those willing to navigate the intricacies of AI and turn them into tools for positive impact. Your journey is just beginning—may it be as enlightening and rewarding as the destination itself promises to be.

References

6 AI myths debunked. (2019, November 5). Gartner. https://ww
w.gartner.com/smarterwithgartner/5-ai-myths-debunked

Berry, I. (2021, October 27). *10 Ways AI Can Used in Homes.*
Aimagazine.com. https://aimagazine.com/top10/10-ways-ai-
can-used-homes

Craig, L. (2024). *What Is Artificial Intelligence (AI)?* TechTarget.
https://www.techtarget.com/searchenterpriseai/definition/A
I-Artificial-Intelligence

Coursera. (2022, August 11). *AI vs. Deep Learning vs. Machine
Learning: Beginner's Guide.* Coursera. https://www.coursera.o
rg/articles/ai-vs-deep-learning-vs-machine-learning-begi
nners-guide

Discover the Differences Between AI vs. Machine Learning vs. Deep

Learning. (n.d.). Simplilearn.com. https://www.simplilearn.com/tutorials/artificial-intelligence-tutorial/ai-vs-machine-learning-vs-deep-learning

Debunking 5 artificial intelligence myths. (2024). Carlson School of Management. https://carlsonschool.umn.edu/graduate/resources/debunking-5-artificial-intelligence-myths

Exploring the Differences Between Narrow AI, General AI, and Superintelligent AI | Institute of Data. (2023, October 6). https://www.institutedata.com/us/blog/exploring-the-differences-between-narrow-ai-general-ai-and-superintelligent-ai/

Larkin, Z. (2022, November 16). *General AI vs Narrow AI.* Levity.ai. https://levity.ai/blog/general-ai-vs-narrow-ai

Stryker, C., & Kavlakoglu, E. (2024, August 9). *What Is Artificial Intelligence (AI)?* IBM. https://www.ibm.com/think/topics/artificial-intelligence

Vina, A. (2025). *A Look at Daily Life with AI-Enabled Smart Home Solutions.* Ultralytics.com. https://www.ultralytics.com/blog/a-look-at-daily-life-with-ai-enabled-smart-home-solutions

Hosokawa, G. (2024, January 3). *How AI Improves Audience Engagement For Streaming Services*. Salesforce. https://www .salesforce.com/blog/audience-engagement-for-streaming- services/

Illia Termeno. (2025, January 30). *Optimize Comfort & Efficiency with Smart Thermostats | Hospitable*. Hospitable.com. https://hospitable.com/smart-thermostats-launch/

Key Features and Uses of AI Voice Assistants. (2025). Www.ema.co. https://www.ema.co/additional-blogs/addition-blogs/key-f eatures-and-uses-of-ai-voice-assistants

Mehta, J. (2023, November 17). *The benefits of personalized product recommendations for website users*. Abmatic.ai. https://a bmatic.ai/blog/benefits-of-personalized-product-recomme ndations-for-website-users

Rands, L. (2025, January 16). *4 Ways AI is Changing Online Shopping Forever*. Finch.com; Finch. https://finch.com/blog/4- ways-ai-changing-online-shopping-forever

Sharma, R. (2024, October 7). *Markovate*. Markovate. https://markovate.com/ai-recommendation-systems/

Smart Thermostats: Enhancing Comfort and Efficiency. (2023). Globalheatingairconditioning.com. https://www.globalhea tingairconditioning.com/blog/smart-thermostats-enhance-comfort/

The Sosa Insurance Group. (2019). Thesosainsurancegroup.com. https://thesosainsurancegroup.com/how-ai-voice-assistant s-are-revolutionizing-our-lives/

The Future of Home Automation: Voice Control Systems for 2024. (2024). Hnkparts.com. https://www.hnkparts.com/blog/pos t/the-future-of-home-automation-voice-control-systems? srsltid=AfmBOopeie5ZnfM-y-18NGs76_8sIKEg1ooCgO-8dd ItlU-i7_e6BN6i

Westlake, M. (2025, February 17). *How AI is Transforming Smart Homes in 2025 and Beyond.* Gearbrain. https://www.gearbrain. com/ai-smart-home-automation-devices-2671168897.htm l

Automated Vehicles for Safety | NHTSA. (2021). Www.nhtsa.gov; National Highway Traffic Safety Administration. https://www. nhtsa.gov/vehicle-safety/automated-vehicles-safety

Koch, R. (2022, July 7). *AI in Traffic Management: Artificial Intelligence solves traffic control issues.* Clickworker.com. https://w

ww.clickworker.com/customer-blog/artificial-intelligence-road-traffic/

MacCarthy, M. (2024, July 31). *The evolving safety and policy challenges of self-driving cars.* Brookings. https://www.brookings.edu/articles/the-evolving-safety-and-policy-challenges-of-self-driving-cars/

Rambus Press. (2022, June 9). *SAE levels of automation in cars simply explained (+Image).* Rambus. https://www.rambus.com/blogs/driving-automation-levels/

Sitaram. (2024, April 12). *Exploring the Role of AI in Self Driving Cars.* Appventurez. https://www.appventurez.com/blog/ai-in-self-driving-cars

Srivastava, S. (2023, December 1). *AI in Transportation: Benefits, Use Cases, and Examples.* Appinventiv. https://appinventiv.com/blog/ai-in-transportation/

SAE International. (2021, May 3). *SAE levels of driving automation^{TM} refined for clarity and international audience.* SAE International. https://www.sae.org/blog/sae-j3016-update

Sheikh Sameer. (2025, February 14). *AI in Transportation: Application, Benefits, and Use Cases.* Apptunix Blog. https://www.apptunix.com/blog/ai-in-transportation/

Tselentis, D. I., Papadimitriou, E., & van Gelder, P. (2023, June 1). *The usefulness of artificial intelligence for safety assessment of different transport modes.* Accident Analysis & Prevention. https://doi.org/10.1016/j.aap.2023.107034

AI Predictive Analytics in Healthcare: What Is It & Benefits. (2024). Keragon.com. https://www.keragon.com/blog/ai-predictive-analytics-in-healthcare

Alowais, S. A., Alghamdi, S. S., Alsuhebany, N., Alqahtani, T., Alshaya, A., Almohareb, S. N., Aldairem, A., Alrashed, M., Saleh, K. B., Badreldin, H. A., Yami, A., Harbi, S. A., & Albekairy, A. M. (2023). *Revolutionizing Healthcare: The Role Of Artificial Intelligence In Clinical Practice.* BMC Medical Education; BioMed Central. https://doi.org/10.1186/s12909-023-04698-z

Bajwa, J., Munir, U., Nori, A., & Williams, B. (2021). *Artificial Intelligence in healthcare: Transforming the Practice of Medicine.* Future Healthcare Journal; NCBI. https://doi.org/10.7861/fhj.2021-0095

Bhandari, A. (2024, October 29). *Revolutionizing Radiology With*

Artificial Intelligence. Cureus; Cureus, Inc. https://doi.org/10.7 759/cureus.72646

Dixon, D., Sattar, H., Moros, N., Kesireddy, S. R., Ahsan, H., Lakkimsetti, M., Fatima, M., Doshi, D., Sadhu, K., & Hassan, M. J. (2024, May 9). *Unveiling the Influence of AI Predictive Analytics on Patient Outcomes: A Comprehensive Narrative Review.* Cureus. https://doi.org/10.7759/cureus.59954

Jafleh, E. A., Alnaqbi, F. A., Almaeeni, H. A., Faqeeh, S., Alzaabi, M. A., & Al Zaman, K. (2024, September 8). *The Role of Wearable Devices in Chronic Disease Monitoring and Patient Care: A Comprehensive Review.* Cureus. https://doi.org/10.7759/cure us.68921

Kaur, J. (2024, October 22). *Ethical Considerations and Bias in Computer Vision (CV).* Xenonstack.com; XenonStack. https://do i.org/1004087609/1739605800683

Khalifa, M., & Albadawy, M. (2024). *AI in diagnostic imaging: Revolutionising accuracy and efficiency.* Computer Methods and Programs in Biomedicine Update; Elsevier BV. https://doi.org/10.1016/j.cmpbup.2024.100146

(2024). Qapla.io. https://www.qapla.io/blog/customer-experi ence/ai-for-customer-retention/

About Us. (2024, July 3). Intelemark. https://www.intelemark. com/blog/role-of-ai-in-customer-retention-strategy/

AI Workflow Automation: What is it and How Does It Work? (2025). Moveworks.com. https://www.moveworks.com/us/en/resou rces/blog/what-is-ai-workflow-automation-impacts-busin ess-processes

Globe, G. (2024, September 28). *Effective Homepage Web Design for Engaging Visitors- Positive trends making it successful 2024 2024 2024.* GO-Globe. https://doi.org/1053633.277

McGrath, A. (2024, July 11). *AI in operations management.* Ibm.com. https://www.ibm.com/think/topics/ai-in-operati ons-management

Rafalski, K. (2023, April 19). *Instant Assistance: How AI Chatbots Are Improving Customer Service.* Www.netguru.com. https://ww w.netguru.com/blog/ai-chatbots-improving-customer-serv ice

R, S. P. (2024, October 18). *Embracing the Future of Data Analytics: Key Drivers.* Acceldata.io; acceldata. https://www.acceldata.i o/blog/future-of-data-analytics-ai-real-time-intelligence- and-advanced-insights

Takyar, A. (2024, January 24). *Harnessing AI for operational efficiency.* LeewayHertz - AI Development Company. https://w ww.leewayhertz.com/ai-for-operational-efficiency/

The State of AI in Business Intelligence and Analytics. (2025, November 6). William & Mary; Raymond A. Mason School of Business, William & Mary. https://online.mason.w m.edu/blog/the-state-of-ai-in-business-intelligence-and-analytics

Why RPA? Exploring the Benefits of Robotic Process Automation | Thoughtful. (n.d.). Www.thoughtful.ai. https://www.thou ghtful.ai/blog/why-rpa-exploring-the-benefits-of-robotic-process-automation-rpa

12 AI Research Tools to Drive Knowledge Exploration | DigitalOcean. (2024). Digitalocean.com. https://www.digitalocean.com/res ources/articles/ai-research-tools

AI research tools for for Academics and Researchers. (2025). Litmaps.com. https://www.litmaps.com/learn/best-ai-rese arch-tools

Bullock, M. (2024, December 20). *How AI Can Tailor Gamifica-tion to Individual Learning Styles.* Spinify. https://spinify.com/ blog/how-ai-can-tailor-gamification-to-individual-learni ng-styles/

Constantino, T. (2024, September 19). *Students Learned Twice As Much With AI Tutor Than Typical Lectures.* Forbes. https://www.forbes.com/sites/torconstantino/2024/09/18/students-learned-twice-as-much-with-ai-tutor-than-typical-lectures/

Hegwood, V. (2023, March 7). *6 Student Progress Monitoring Tools & How They Work.* Www.prodigygame.com. https://www.prodigygame.com/main-en/blog/student-progress-monitoring-tools/

Labadze, L., Grigolia, M., & Machaidze, L. (2023, October 31). *Role of AI Chatbots in education: Systematic Literature Review.* International Journal of Educational Technology in Higher Education; Springer Nature. https://doi.org/10.1186/s41239-023-00426-1

Marsh, B. (2024, October 22). *15 Benefits of AI in Education.* RTS Labs. https://rtslabs.com/benefits-of-ai-in-education

Meehir, K. (2023, June 6). *How AI Is Personalizing Education For Every Student.* ELearning Industry. https://elearningindustry.com/how-ai-is-personalizing-education-for-every-student

Murray, F. (2024, September 27). *Use of Big Data for Adaptive Learning: How Analytics are Shaping Specialized Education*. Tech Research Online. https://techresearchonline.com/blog/big-data-for-adaptive-learning/

Progress Monitoring | Center on Multi-Tiered Systems of Support. (n.d.). Mtss4success.org. https://mtss4success.org/essential-components/progress-monitoring

Adams, T. (2024, December 4). *How AI Fuels Gaming Innovation - Ted Adams - Medium*. Medium. https://medium.com/@ted.adams38/how-ai-fuels-gaming-innovation-e7cdefbb1b3b

AI's Impact on Modern Filmmaking. (2024, November 7). Vitrina. https://vitrina.ai/blog/ais-transformative-role-in-filmmaking/

API4AI. (2025, February 15). *AI Trends Shaping Entertainment in 2025 | by API4AI | Medium*. Medium. https://medium.com/@API4AI/top-ai-trends-transforming-the-entertainment-industry-in-2025-d7b1d0e94d40

Capitol Technology University. (2023, May 30). *The Ethical Considerations of Artificial Intelligence*. Www.captechu.edu; Capitol Technology University. https://www.captechu.edu/blog/ethical-considerations-of-artificial-intelligence

Chow, A. (2023, December 4). *How AI Is Transforming Music.* TIME. https://time.com/6340294/ai-transform-music-2023/

Girimonte, M. (2024, October 29). *How AI is Redefining Interactive Storytelling.* Voices. https://www.voices.com/blog/ai-interactive-storytelling/

Paul, J. (2024, November 14). *ETHICAL IMPLICATIONS OF AI IN BUSINESS.* https://www.researchgate.net/publication/385782 217_ETHICAL_IMPLICATIONS_OF_AI_IN_BUSINESS

Sahota, N. (2024, March 8). *The AI Takeover In Cinema: How Movie Studios Use Artificial Intelligence.* Forbes. https://www.f orbes.com/sites/neilsahota/2024/03/08/the-ai-takeover-in-cinema-how-movie-studios-use-artificial-intelligence/

The CEO Views, & The CEO Views. (2025, January 18). *The CEO Views.* The CEO Views. https://theceoviews.com/how-artificial-intelligence-is-changing-computer-games-from-smart-npcs-to-procedural-world-generation/

semancik, A. (2024, April 3). *How AI is transforming the creative economy and music industry.* OHIO News. https://www.ohio.e du/news/2024/04/how-ai-transforming-creative-economy -music-industry

Bowie, J. (2024, December 16). *The Impact of Artificial Intelligence: Transforming Our World.* Pickl.AI. https://www.pickl.ai/blog/impact-of-artificial-intelligence/

Codemotion. (2024, May 13). *Don't Get Yourself Replaced: Top 8 Emerging AI Jobs.* Codemotion Magazine. https://www.codemotion.com/magazine/it-careers/dont-get-yourself-replaced-top-8-emerging-ai-jobs/

Caylor, B. (2024, April 5). *5 Essential AI Skills for Students in the Modern Workforce.* Medium; Medium. https://bartcaylor.medium.com/5-essential-ai-skills-for-students-in-the-modern-workforce-1f00ec317e09

Capitol Technology University. (2023, May 30). *The Ethical Considerations of Artificial Intelligence.* Www.captechu.edu; Capitol Technology University. https://www.captechu.edu/blog/ethical-considerations-of-artificial-intelligence

Dev1. (2025, February 8). *Enhancing remote teamwork with AI in virtual environments.* Hyperspace^{mv} - the Metaverse for Business Platform. https://hyperspace.mv/enhancing-remote-teamwork-with-ai-in-virtual-environments/

How AI is Shaping the Future of Remote Work and Virtual Collab-

oration. (2024, November 13). FPGA Insights. https://fpgai nsights.com/artificial-intelligence/how-ai-is-shaping-the-future-of-remote-work/

Lumenalta. (2024). *Ethical Considerations of AI: Fairness, transparency, and Frameworks | Future of Responsible AI | Lumenalta.* Lumenalta. https://doi.org/1019928/1920x728/4568b12430

Rashid, A. B., & Kausik, A. K. (2024, August 1). *AI Revolutionizing Industries Worldwide: a Comprehensive Overview of Its Diverse Applications.* Hybrid Advances; Elsevier BV. https://doi.org/10.1016/j.hybadv.2024.100277

Top 10 Skills Employers Are Looking for in 2024. (2024, January 16). Www.stjohns.edu. https://www.stjohns.edu/news-media/johnnies-blog/top-skills-employers-are-looking-for

What Jobs will Artificial Intelligence Create? | Workplace Conversations | AIM WA. (2024). Workplace Conversations. https://aimw a.com/wctm/innovation/at-work/what-jobs-will-artificial-intelligence-create/

Beginner's Guide to AI Project Resources | Restackio. (2024). Restack.io. https://www.restack.io/p/beginners-guide-to-a rtificial-intelligence-answer-ai-project-resources-cat-ai

QuadC. (2023, September 12). *Enhancing Collaboration and Support with Online Learning Communities.* Quadc.io; QuadC. https://www.quadc.io/blog/enhancing-collaboration-and-support-with-online-learning-communities

Webinar recap: Demystifying AI for communities | Khoros. (2023). Khoros.com. https://khoros.com/blog/webinar-recap-demystifying-ai-and-communities

fast.ai Course Forums. (2017, November 9). *Resources Master Thread.* Fast.ai Course Forums. https://forums.fast.ai/t/resources-master-thread/7591

Collina, L., Mostafa Sayyadi, & Provitera, M. (2023, November 6). *Critical Issues About A.I. Accountability Answered.* California Management Review Insights. https://cmr.berkeley.edu/2023/11/critical-issues-about-a-i-accountability-answered/

DigitalOcean. (2024). *Addressing AI Bias: Real-World Challenges and How to Solve Them | DigitalOcean.* Digitalocean.com. https://www.digitalocean.com/resources/articles/ai-bias

Ferrara, E. (2023, December 26). *Fairness and Bias in Artificial Intelligence: A Brief Survey of Sources, Impacts, and Mitigation Strategies.* Sci; Multidisciplinary Digital Publishing Institute.

https://doi.org/10.3390/sci6010003

Fazlioglu, M. (2023, November 8). *International Association of Privacy Professionals*. Iapp.org. https://iapp.org/news/a/training-ai-on-personal-data-scraped-from-the-web

How to Mitigate Bias in AI Systems Through AI Governance. (2024). Holisticai.com. https://www.holisticai.com/blog/mitigate-bias-ai-systems-governance

Mirko Zorz. (2024, November 7). *How AI will shape the next generation of cyber threats - Help Net Security.* Help Net Security. https://www.helpnetsecurity.com/2024/11/07/buzz-hillestad-prismatic-ai-driven-attacks/

Radanliev, P. (2025, February 7). *AI Ethics: Integrating Transparency, Fairness, and Privacy in AI Development.* Applied Artificial Intelligence; Informa UK Limited. https://doi.org/10.1080/08839514.2025.2463722

Ryan, M., Antoniou, J., Brooks, L., Jiya, T., Macnish, K., & Stahl, B. (2021, March 8). *Research and Practice of AI Ethics: A Case Study Approach Juxtaposing Academic Discourse with Organisational Reality.* Science and Engineering Ethics. https://doi.org/10.1007/s11948-021-00293-x

Stevens, J. (2023, August 4). *AI Accountability: Who's Responsible When AI Goes Wrong?* Emerge Digital. https://emerge.digital/resources/ai-accountability-whos-responsible-when-ai-goes-wrong/

Varsha, P. S. (2023, April). *How can we manage biases in artificial intelligence systems – A systematic literature review.* International Journal of Information Management Data Insights. https://doi.org/10.1016/j.jjimei.2023.100165

Cinelli, M., Morales, G. D. F., Galeazzi, A., Quattrociocchi, W., & Starnini, M. (2021, February 23). *The Echo Chamber Effect on Social Media.* Proceedings of the National Academy of Sciences; PNAS. https://doi.org/10.1073/pnas.2023301118

Keenan, N. (2023, October 23). *The impact of AI on social media, pros & cons | Born Social.* Www.bornsocial.co. https://www.bornsocial.co/post/impact-of-ai-on-social-media

Manning, S. (2024, July 3). *AI's impact on income inequality in the US.* Brookings. https://www.brookings.edu/articles/ais-impact-on-income-inequality-in-the-us/

Pavel, B., Ke, I., Spirtas, M., Ryseff, J., Sabbag, L., Smith, G., Scholl, K., & Lumpkin, D. (2023, November 3). *AI and Geopolitics: How Might AI Affect the Rise and Fall of Nations?*

Www.rand.org. https://www.rand.org/pubs/perspectives/PEA3034-1.html

Renda, A., Wyckoff, A. W., Kerry, C. F., & Meltzer, J. P. (2025, February 10). *Network architecture for global AI policy.* Brookings. https://www.brookings.edu/articles/network-architecture-for-global-ai-policy/

Sharps, S. (2024). *The Impact of AI on the Labour Market.* Institute.global; Tony Blair Institute. https://institute.global/insights/economic-prosperity/the-impact-of-ai-on-the-labour-market

Schellekens, P., & Skilling, D. (2024, October 17). *Three Reasons Why AI May Widen Global Inequality.* Center for Global Development. https://www.cgdev.org/blog/three-reasons-why-ai-may-widen-global-inequality

The Impact of AI on the Job Market: Navigating the Evolution of Work. (2024). Launchconsulting.com. https://www.launchconsulting.com/posts/the-impact-of-ai-on-the-job-market-navigating-the-evolution-of-work

The Role of AI in Startups and Venture Capital + Top VCs Investing in AI. (2024, August 13). Visible.vc. https://visible.vc/blog/ai-investors/

Wall, D. (2025, January 2). *Impact of AI Startups on Venture Capital Trends.* Fundz.net; Fundz, LLC. http://www.fundz.ne t/venture-capital-blog/impact-of-ai-startups-on-venture-capital-trends

Cruz, J. (2022, April 29). *CLOSED: Call for Papers: Special Issue on Next-Gen AI: Advances and Applications Shaping the Future.* IEEE Computer Society. https://www.computer.org/digital-library/magazine/it/cfp-next-gen-ai/

How Artificial Intelligence Helps the Environment & Sustainability | Perch Energy. (n.d.). Www.perchenergy.com. https://w ww.perchenergy.com/blog/innovation/artificial-intelligence -environment-sustainability

Money Tent. (2024, April 26). *20 Visionary Technologies That Will Reshape Society.* Medium. https://medium.com/@money tent/20-visionary-technologies-that-will-reshape-society-86fe17d0e75d

PWC. (2022). *The Essential Eight Technologies.* PwC. https://ww w.pwc.com/us/en/tech-effect/emerging-tech/essential-eigh t-technologies.html

QIAN, Y., SIAU, K. L., & NAH, F. F. (2024, January 1). *Societal Impacts of Artificial Intelligence: Ethical, Legal, and*

Governance Issues. Societal Impacts; Elsevier BV. https://doi.org/10.1016/j.socimp.2024.100040

Se, K. (2024, December 24). 🔲*#81: Key AI Concepts to Follow in 2025 - Ksenia Se - Medium.* Medium. https://kseniase.medium.com/80-whats-in-2025-from-elad-gil-franc%CC%A7ois-chollet-maxime-labonne-swyx-and-others-17b732b16e1c

Team, A. (2024, November 12). *Navigating AI Ethical Issues in Workforce Management: Balancing Innovation and Integrity.* Getaura.ai. https://blog.getaura.ai/ai-ethical-issues

The Rise of Physical AI: Bridging Artificial Intelligence with the Tangible World. (2025). Profbanafa.com. https://www.profbanafa.com/2025/01/the-rise-of-physical-ai-bridging.html

UNEP. (2022, November 7). *How artificial intelligence is helping tackle environmental challenges.* UNEP. https://www.unep.org/news-and-stories/story/how-artificial-intelligence-helping-tackle-environmental-challenges

WEBIT_Admin, & Webit. (2024, September 12). *Webit Blog.* Webit Blog. https://blog.webit.org/2024/09/12/visionary-review-of-top-10-tech-trends/